MONOLOGUES

FOR

MEN

BY

MEN

Volume Two

EDITED BY GARY GARRISON
& MICHAEL WRIGHT

HEINEMANN
Portsmouth, NH

This volume is dedicated to Lisa Barnett,
our editor at Heinemann,
a great lover of books, people, theatre . . . and us.

Heinemann
A division of Reed Elsevier Inc.
361 Hanover Street
Portsmouth, NH 03801–3912
www.heinemanndrama.com

Offices and agents throughout the world

© 2003 by Heinemann

Performance rights material can be found on page 162.

Library of Congress Cataloging-in-Publication Data
Monologues for men by men : volume two / edited by Gary Garrison
& Michael Wright.
       p. cm.
    Volume One: ISBN 0-325-00374-2
    Volume Two: ISBN 0-325-00559-1 (alk. paper)
       1. Monologues. 2. Acting. 3. American drama—20th century.
    4. Men—Drama. I. Garrison, Gary. II. Wright, Michael, 1945–

PN2080 .M537 2002
808.82'45—dc21

                                2001051628

Editor: Lisa A. Barnett
Production: Elizabeth Valway
Cover design: Darci Mehall, Aureo Design
Typesetter: Tom Allen, Pear Graphic Design
Manufacturing: Steve Bernier

Printed in the United States of America on acid-free paper
07 06 05 04 03 DA 1 2 3 4 5

Contents

Introduction

A Sort of Monologue

BY MICHAEL WRIGHT

So this is 1999, Washington, DC, and there's me and Gary and some other writers, and we're signing books for Heinemann in their booth at the annual ATHE Conference, and Gary picks up one of Tori Haring-Smith's "monologues for women by women" volumes, looks at me and says (portentous kettle drums here):

"We could do this."

And I agree, and we pitch it to Lisa Barnett, our editor, and next thing we know we have the book out, and Heinemann is asking for a second volume. And so here we are, easy as cake.

Well, not quite.

For me, the first volume was a revelation in the way it came together and in the way Gary approached it. I hadn't thought beyond good words from good playwrights for good actors to make good with, but Gary had his eye on another level: What it means to be a male these days. And that opened up a whole realm of thinking my brain hadn't gotten to, and the people who've responded to the book have fallen into two major areas: (1) thanks for the good monos, dudes; and (2) thanks for taking on these notions of maleness, dudes. (I'm throwing in the "dudes" part—gives it that ring of authentic male-speak.)

So here I am now, at the keyboard, Buddha sitting smiling atop my computer monitor, feeling yet another wave of wonder at what this project has become. Because this time we've tapped into a new thing, and several new things have tapped into us.

The thing we've tapped into is international playwrights, for which I will take responsibility (and praise—Buddha shakes his patient head at me: attachment to ego, oh dear). In the past decade, I've been luckier than Lou Gehrig to encounter a number of opportunities for which I could travel to other countries to work with, learn from, and talk with playwrights from cultures utterly different from my own. When Heinemann asked for Volume Two, I immediately wanted to bring in these guys from other places; buyers of this volume can read and work on monologues by playwrights from Australia, Singapore, Sweden, Canada, and the United Kingdom.

What's intriguing is that you'll find they're not "alien" to our U.S. experience of maledom. That beat seems to go on around the globe and the songs from the first volume continue to be about identity, confusion, love, sex, our fathers, work . . .

But what I'm tripping on even more is what tapped into us: first—horribly, sadly—the unthinkable: the terrorist acts in the U.S.; and second, the seeming rise of an interest in the architecture of the page in some of our playwrights.

As to the events of 9/11, there is everything and nothing to say. The misguided individuals who perpetrated those horrendous acts against humanity thought perhaps they'd still the free voices of thinkers, artists, writers, but the opposite has happened. Around the world, the anniversary of 9/11 saw readings of new works in memory of the events in gentle but emphatic defiance of their inhumane deeds. This volume, as well, presents a number of monologues that respond to the attacks. Some are grouped in a particular segment, but others throughout the book are tinged with the effects and aftermath of the attacks.

(I stop writing for a moment in sad reflection over 9/11, but just outside my door theatre students are playing and laughing. Their life force reminds me to push on. We will all re-meet 9/11 again and again in our lives; it's the pushing-on that matters.)

The 9/11-related monologues remind us of the power of the single voice to say no to terror or threat or political hypocrisy, and be heard, and set off answering echoes.

The second unexpected element is an intriguing development in contemporary theatre, which is writers using a sort of "page architecture" to create the look of their play's feelings. This architecture does some very cool things, by my reckoning: It does away with punctuation in many cases, creating a distinctive sense of phrasing for the actor (meaning that the actor can just play the work line by line, or run the lines together and create his own sense of punctuation).

It also hearkens the writer's work back to the essential roots of theatre in poetry. These monologues look like poems! And I personally find that exciting because it pushes the monologue form and poetry forward at the same time.

(What the hell does that mean—I imagine some reader asking.)

Well, it means that we are reminded that poetry is not just for the eye and the page, but for speaking aloud so that the sound becomes as large a part of the experience as does stuff like metaphor and word choice and other literary aspects.

Poetry is no more literature than theatre is: Without the human voice, it's just words on a page. And the instrumentation of the human voice is about breath and hearing and sharing—it's experiential, immediate, in-the-present. In other words, it is theatre.

And all theatre is essentially poetic because it is metaphorical, so the monologues are not just talking to talk but talking to raise questions, open doors, shine a light, test a foundation, fight a battle, crumble a fortress.

Which brings us back to a point I made in the last book, but from a different angle: If the actor is to succeed with a given monologue, it comes as much from trying to get a sense of the spark, impulse, hiccup that compelled the writer to write the thing, as it does from anything else.

Writer and actor form a joined being through the

monologue. In performance, the audience becomes a third element of that joined being. This is true of all monologues, even those that are not architecturally constructed (though the standard form is also architectural, isn't it?).

In the case of the architectural monologues, this joining comes from the way in which the architecture exposes the ribs and guts of the piece. Each line or phrase really reveals the exact thought as the playwright struggled to write it; those individual thoughts don't get swallowed up in a lot of words, like in this paragraph. To lay it out visually/architecturally, the preceding sentence would look like this:

> Each line or phrase
> really
> reveals the exact thought
> as the playwright struggled to write it
> those individual thoughts don't get
> swallowed up
> in a lot of words . . .

Where does your breath fall in reading those lines out loud? Doesn't the breath, then, create/replace the punctuation? And doesn't this bring thought, word, interpretation, breath, and sound into a unique nexus?

And somehow, then, all the elements in the book form a nexus. Look at how these things criss-cross:

> Maleness
> 9/11
> International voices
> Theatre as poetry
> Poetry as theatre
> The monologue as bonding place between writer and
>   actor
> Page architecture (traditional or not)
> The breath

Performance
Audience
Your thinking right at this moment

For my thinking at this moment, Volume Two strongly suggests that our work has become about running through boundaries. The first volume nibbles at the edge of this, but the world has changed since those good old days.

Our work now—playwrights, actors, audiences, those who write books—is about transcending the day-to-day and moving toward some other level. If I connect with my own maleness, I can better understand yours, and better understand femaleness, and walls tumble. If we can all observe how much of the world has become a literal community of compassion since 9/11, distances and distinctions both fade and become more brilliantly emphatic at once. If I can recognize your difference and my own difference, our sameness becomes manifest. If I can craft my creation in a way that generates a more immediate, intuitive, heart-ful connection with your reading and performed interpretation of it, then a kind of oneness obtains, and so on.

Phew, I'm going in a thousand directions with this. Tripping, like I said.

What staggers me most, in the end, is that from an electronic firing in some segment of the porridge we carry in our heads, we somehow arrive at this book, this work of many hands. And we are a collective, gathered in the same sort of ephemeral fashion in which all theatre occurs—here now, then gone—but given the illusion of permanence through publication, the awarding of an ISBN code, and so on. And these monologues are what we're thinking and concerned about, in a brave new world; new voices in sometimes new forms, addressing all that remains and all that has changed.

* * *

A few final words:

The majority of the labor has fallen, once again, on Gary's shoulders. He organized the monologues into related groupings and took on the burden of introducing each group, organizing the critical information, inputting the creative work and data into the manuscript, and so on. That the first volume was a revelation is due to Gary's thinking and work in developing the book beyond just nice speeches. The quality of Volume Two is also Gary's creation, in large part, in tandem with the writers and my own spurts of assistance. (He might not like that I've written this, but since I get to do the intro, it's my choice so he'll have to live with this praise.)

The monologue form still intrigues us. We've done royal battle with some of our writers to get their work active and in the present, when their initial choice was to write stories spoken in third-person, past-tense narration. Perhaps one day we might anthologize those kinds of narratives, but we still feel our mission is to serve a vast population of actors who need new characters to explore. But, we are still uncertain about who exactly buys this kind of book, so we're open to your feedback and input, which leads to the last point.

We'd like to hear from you about this book and the first volume. Are there areas our playwrights haven't explored that you feel need addressing? Have the monologues been useful? If so, how? What is your feeling about the architectural page form? Get in touch. Michael Wright: *michael-wright@utulsa.edu*. Gary Garrison: *boxerman10003@yahoo.com*.

Best of luck with your creative work; we're thrilled to share ours with you.

The Ache

Subject introductions written by Gary Garrison

Forgive my darkness, 'cause you know there's nothing more I like than the light. But there's an ache in me when you're not around.

In the five minutes you leave a room, or the five days you go on a business trip, or the five years you check out of our relationship to see what life on the outside feels like, an ache grows in me that buckles me at the knees and brings me crashing forward on top of my head. Then: blackout. Half of my city is shut down. Maybe more.

Yeah, I mean, the necessary systems still operate. I can breathe, piss, gulp, blink, pick a pen up, set a plate down. Thank God for automatic systems. But it's not much more than that. Head's frozen. Heart's an ice-brick. Soul's just a darkness.

So there I lay, ebbing life from the pulse at my temples, waiting for you to walk back through the door. And then you do. And I get upright again. But each time the climb back from horizontal to vertical gets harder and harder. Each time the generator takes a little longer to kick back in. Each time the electricity that should be free-flowing through my city creeps at a snail's pace back into high performance. And I worry that one day it'll never get there. One day I'll be a city that can't break its one-third darkness.

I don't know what the hell I'm trying to say, sweetheart. But I want to stop worrying that these absences between us feel like the tiniest little death—be it five minutes, five days, five years, or in that instant when our fingers intertwine and I have that urge to say, "Honey, that's not holding my hand; that's just laying your hand in mine."

The Paper Bag

AARON COATES

HERB sits in the passenger seat of a car, with a paper-bagged lunch.

HERB: Before I go, Honey, you should know that I haven't eaten my lunch for several weeks—and let me tell you why. Let me get it out! Don't say anything. Just . . . let me get it out.

I appreciate that you make a lunch for me every day. The thought is *great*, the effort is *great*. But I have to tell you: a few weeks ago, I spread it all out in front of me in the staff room like always and I looked at it. Then, I threw it out. I know there are children starving in third world countries and homeless people and students and unemployed actors who would kill for good wholesome food like that, but I realized something important. See, you've packed me the same thing every day since I can remember. Bologna and cheese on white bread, a Gala apple, and a chocolate chip granola bar. Looking at that lunch, I realized that we're *settling down*. We're *finding a groove*. And that's about the worst thing we could do.

We've always talked about—right?—about how many couples we know that are so cold to each other because they've fallen into a routine. And now we have too. The lunch made it all clear. Our holidays, our nights out, our conversations, our sex life, our sleeping patterns, our clothing, our television habits: they're all "Bologna and cheese on white bread, a Gala apple, and a chocolate chip granola bar." You see? They're all falling into a pattern. It has to end. And the end starts with the lunch you packed me today. I'm not going to take it. I'm going to eat at Papa Pear's. I'm going to have . . . I don't know what I'm going to have! But I think that *that's* happiness. So, Honey, I'm going to leave the lunch here and in exchange I want you to give me a kiss. How about it? The lunch . . . for a kiss.

Longing

DEAN CORRIN

A guy who's not as young as he used to be, in a motel room.

GUY: I wish you wouldn't make me have to ask you. That it didn't always have to be up to me to bring it up. It must be on your mind sometimes. If just once in a while it could be your idea . . . if you could just make the suggestion . . . then I'd feel like you really want to. That it wasn't just your duty or your obligation. Because right now, I'm almost afraid to ask. Like I'm not supposed to bring it up. Like I'm being too demanding. And then if you say "no" you're upset and I'm pissed off, but if you don't want to and you say "yes" it's like I'm forcing you.

Now don't get me wrong. I don't mind driving. I like driving. I'm happy to drive most of the time. Just about all of the time. But there are times when I really wish you'd take the wheel for a while. It's been two thousand miles in the last week. I've driven every single mile. On the highway, in town. Day and night. Traffic or no traffic. Across Ohio. Through Pennsylvania. I would just like, for one day, to sit on the passenger side. To do the things that you do. Look out at the mountains. Watch the people on the street. Look for a restaurant we could stop at.

But I've got to keep my eyes on the road. My hands on the wheel. Worry about that guy in the station wagon who won't stay in his lane or the semi bearing down on me when I'm stuck between a minivan and a delivery truck. Or wondering what happens if that school bus grazes the tailpipe laying in the middle of the road and sends it flying up so that it crashes through the windshield or slides underneath us and pierces the gas tank.

And then I glance over at you and you're reading a book. Or sleeping. With your seat tipped back. For the last two thousand miles I've been sitting perfectly upright, checking the rearview mirror every three seconds, watching the temperature gauge creep up and calculating difference in the gas mileage with the air conditioner on or off. I wonder what it would be like to recline the seat and close my eyes. To fall asleep in Ohio and awaken in Illinois, having passed through Indiana as a dream. To peer down into the valleys and observe the villages of Massachusetts.

But you never offer. I never ask. We never speak of it. Safety belted in our seats. I adjust the rearview mirror. You operate the temperature controls. I turn on the headlights while you search for a radio station when the signal begins to fade. We drive ahead into the night. Counting down the miles as the markers blur by. You to my right. Me to your left. Looking ahead. Glancing behind. Looking ahead. Knowing only what lies before as far as the high beams reach. Speeding into that canopy of light. I wait for you to offer. I long for you to take the wheel. "Maybe at the rest stop," I think. "Maybe when we stop for gas." But I hear the pace of your breathing slow, the even rhythm of your sleep. It's too late now. It's too late now to ask. Maybe tomorrow. Maybe tomorrow you'll offer to drive. And let me tune the radio until I find a song we both remember. A song we both can sing along to as we drive into the dark.

Jonathon and Stuart

ANTON DUDLEY

JONATHON and Stuart sit on a Park Bench.

JONATHON: I don't know why I came here, I don't like parks. I went into this other one once, a lot like this one but not— and—it was Fall, you know, crispy and cool and—an acorn, but bigger, like a chestnut or something, fell on my head. . . . It hurt. Then I found a leaf. Like it was orange like fire and I picked it up and had this feeling like when you're touching something you know you shouldn't. Like the first time you found your mother's underwear drawer and you fondled her bras. It was like that—this leaf—this orange, orange leaf—and I'm fixated, I'm drawn in by "the magic of Nature" or whatever—and like five minutes later I got this really bad rash on my hand. . . . Parks. And I don't like squirrels. Like rats only with salon privileges. But this park—this specific park—I could probably learn to like it. For you, Stuart. Well, because of you, I suppose.

I could like this particular park. It's full of bugs, but— bugs, I have come to learn, are high in protein—almost ALL protein in fact, no carbs at all—and, unlike steak and pork, they're not chewy, but crunchy. Crunchy like candies or a crisp chocolate. Like a dish of frosted bon-bons set out for fidgeting fingers at the doctor's office or while waiting for a hostess at a party where you've arrived too early. Not that I eat bugs, but I find that sort of fascinating. All that stuff I just said about them? The protein and . . .

But aside from bugs, I like ducks: I don't wear dander or down and my quilts on my bed are made of wool, not feath-ers—I have no qualms with the destruction of sheep: they're silly and stupid and lamb tastes far better than beef, but ducks: ducks I enjoy. The way they walk: thinking they should really fly and when they attempt to fly they know they should really walk—it's their perverse confusion that makes them attractive—and what they are good at is floating: sitting on a pond and simply . . . floating. They are so adept at this task that people have even named these places "Duck Ponds." We don't call fields "Sheep Fields" or sidewalks "People Passages"—but we do say "Duck Ponds" because these ducks have, in their own oblivious little ducky way, come to deserve this. This title. This recognition.

And we laugh at them and make fun of them behind their bills, but what would a park be without ducks—seriously ask yourself—ask any child what's in a park and they'll tell you: trees, ducks and a duck pond—that's what they'll say, it's what I said then—as a child—and it's pretty much what I say now. That and . . . you, Stuart.

Because you're always in this park. Like the ducks. Just sitting here. Lost in your own little world. Floating. Just like the ducks. And I come home at night and sometimes home from work in the day, maybe hoping for a little lunch and a little time together and—you're never there. No. You're here. In this park. Nibbling on bread, just like the ducks, or wandering around aimlessly on the grass. Just like the ducks. Just exactly like those fucky, plucky ducks. I half expect one day to wish you good morning and have you respond with a "quack." And, although that would be at least something. Some response. It would probably still be rather odd. Although odd is something I have come to accept as normal in our odd little seemingly normal relationship. You just might one day turn to me and "quack." Yes, Stuart . . . I half expect that just may happen.

The Night We Met

JEFFERY ELWELL

CARL *stands in the doorway, soaking wet. He's holding a nearly empty bottle of Southern Comfort.* CARL *walks in, closing the door. Jim is seated on the couch.*

CARL: You wanted to know the truth? (*A beat.*) Okay, I'll tell you the truth. No, you wanted the truth and now you're going to hear me out. The truth is it wasn't love at first sight for me. Far from it.

The night we met was the worst night of my entire life. At one point I thought it was going to be my last. That's why I was in the bar on Rush Street that night. I was trying to get drunk so I would have courage enough to kill myself. You want to know why I wanted to kill myself?

Someone rejected me. Just like I've rejected you, Jim. Someone I was in love with, someone who I thought loved me. But I was wrong. She didn't love me. She couldn't have loved me, not the way she had treated me that evening. What should have been the best day of my life turned out to be the worst. We had been going together my entire sophomore year at Northwestern. She was an English major, a senior, and absolutely gorgeous. I had been a perfect gentleman. I mean, we had fooled around some but we had never . . . I had never . . . not until that night . . . and then I couldn't . . . (*Pauses.*) Couldn't do it. Couldn't perform. And Janet . . . She was furious. Told me I had insulted her. Accused me of . . . (*A beat.*) Of being gay. Called me a fag. She said I had to be gay if I wasn't aroused by her . . . I tried to explain but she just got dressed and stormed out . . . she wouldn't listen to me . . . and I started thinking that maybe she was right. . . . I remembered thinking how I found some guys attractive . . . never in a sexual way but it bothered me just the same . . . so I went to the bar. That night. That was the night we met, Jim. And that was why I went home with you that night.

No, look at me goddammit! I want you to face up to the truth. It wasn't love at first sight, Jim. It wasn't anything. Just a refuge in the storm that was my life. But not anymore. I know now what I want. (*Pauses.*)

And that's why we will never be. We have no future. We have no present. We only have the past and it's over. (*Pauses.*)

I need to say this, Jim. I needed to face you and tell you straight out that . . . no punches pulled. You can't control who falls in love with you. I can't. You can't. No one can. You fell in love with me and it didn't work out. I'm sorry. I'm really truly sorry. I know it hurts. I know it drives you crazy. I know it can destroy your life. But we all still want it. It's the hardest goddamn thing in the world to get and it's even harder to keep. But no matter how many times I fail at love, no matter how many times I'm rejected, I'm not going to give up. (*Bends over and kisses Jim on the forehead.*)

And you shouldn't either.

She's Material

BOB FORD

Screenwriter ELLIOT, reeling from a bad break-up, is in his agent's office begging for another couple of weeks to finish off a script he's seriously behind on.

ELLIOT: Work, you know, ha-ha, I can *work* like this? I mean (you're the last person I should be telling this to) I sit, I'm at the keyboard, and you know I have these windows on either side of the monitor—these glorious windows, Upper West Side spread out like, whatever—and all morning, I'm supposed to be writing, I time the commuter ferries. They're right below me, you know where I am in Jersey. They're passing each other back and forth in the middle of the river and I'm like "Whoa, look the fuck out, you're fucking gonna *hit* that guy!" You know, how the angle is, "Look out!" And of course they're really fucking miles apart.

Which is, of course, you know, *Pardon the metaphor.*

Shit I'm a mess.

Thing is, Marty, I asked her. "Is there anything I should know? Should I really come over there?" you know, to see the play. And this isn't exactly small change, I mean for *you* maybe, you know, *life of an agent,* but not for me. This is last-minute tickets to fucking London. And there's been one or two hints of trouble, in the e-mails. One particular line, "I've fallen in *like* with an Englishman"—which is cute, which I just know I'm gonna use sometime. So okay maybe there's a crush, it'll pass. Nevertheless I call her up and I ask point blank, "Should I come over?" Leaving her open to tell me if something's up with the Brit. "Absolutely," she says. "I absolutely want to see you," which is how she said it too. Very matter-of-fact, you know, *Are you kidding? Of course I want to see you.* How am I supposed to know it was a fucking set-up? That in her mind it was over? That in her mind, we'd reached this new so-called *place* . . . I mean, she introduces me to the guy—"this is my writer friend from the states." My *writer* friend?

She's material. That's what you're gonna say, isn't it? She's great material. And I agree, and . . .

Marty, okay, I need two weeks. One act per week. I'm behind, but I'm over this. I mean, I got myself outta the apartment, I got through the tunnel, I negotiated the subway, I survived your fucking receptionist, these are all good signs.

Two weeks, okay? Two weeks?

Shakespeare in Hollywood

KEN LUDWIG

WARNER: Reinhardt?! (*No answer.*) Unbelievable. Max Reinhardt. Mr. Genius. He hires an unknown actor for the leading role, he spends me into the ground, he blackmails me into doing the movie in the first place, and he hides my most expensive actor under papier-mâché! Why don't we just hold a contest in the lobby after each performance: "Guess the star and win a box of popcorn!" I should have my head examined. Of course, I did it all for Lydia. A chorus girl. I'm a 50-year-old mogul and I fell in love with a chorus girl. I'm a walking cliché. On our very first date, she turned to me and said she wanted a starring part in my next movie. I said, "Are you crazy?" She looked at me with those liquid eyes and said, "What's the use of sleeping with an old man unless he makes me a star?" (*Chuckles happily.*)

She's so adorable. O the lengths we men go for the love of a good woman. We make movies, paint pictures, build cathedrals, all for the turn of a head, the rustle of a skirt, a glimpse of that brand new nose she just acquired through plastic surgery. (*Looks off dreamily.*)

If that wonderful girl ever knew how much I love her, she'd make my life a living hell.

Male Pattern

TODD McCULLOUGH

This is disastrous. I can't believe this is happening. Well, no, I can believe it because male pattern, right? Male pattern baldness? Thanks a lot, mom. Thanks for this little genetic gift. Bitch. It is from the mother's side, right? Male pattern? Because I love my mom and I don't wanna call her a bitch unless, you know, unless it's really warranted.

So, but anyway, this is just completely, it's really just an opportune, it's an inopportune moment, essentially, because . . . ah shit . . . because I've started seeing someone. Someone else. Someone other than my . . . spouse. Because things have not exactly been . . . it feels like brother and sister-ish, the whole thing, our living arrangement. It's very sibling-esque. And she's . . . I mean, I still love her, somewhere, on some level, but to say that the thrill is gone would be the understatement of the century. Not only has the flame been extinguished, I'm pretty sure the pilot light's out too.

I know, I'm terrible, huh? The whole thing will be disastrous. I'm an asshole. That's all there is to it. I'm an asshole. Do you think I'm an asshole? No, never mind, I'm an asshole, I know it. I'm a big, huge . . . fucker. But she's really sexy, the woman, and smart and cultured and attractive and sexy and I just think that this is really what I need right now, someone more attuned to my needs than . . . than uh . . . the missus. Jesus, I can't believe I'm saying this . . . 'Til death do us part, or until I get a boner. But anyway, I met her at this party, it was actually a party to celebrate Ken Kerchoff's promotion, and that guy, I mean what a fucker. You know? That position, I busted my ass for three months, three months I busted my ass, and that smarmy little . . . okay, fuck it, fuck him. The woman.

I meet this woman, beautiful long, blonde hair, gorgeous smile, middle management Helen of Troy. And actually, funny enough, I think she used to date Ken, so, you know, we're talking and flirting and it's like, fuck *you* Ken. But we end up out on this balcony and we're both, I mean we've been drinking, and . . . she just . . . she just ran her hand through my hair and looked into my eyes and . . . smiled. And for about four good, solid seconds, I just felt like everything was okay. Ken, my wife, the promotion, all of it was just . . . poof. We went back to her place and made love and after that she just . . . kept running that hand through my hair until I fell asleep. And I think, I mean I really do think that it was probably the closest feeling I've ever had to being back in the womb. It really was just the most secure, comfortable feeling I've had in a long, long time.

And so I guess, I just hope that even with my hair falling out, I hope she still wants to see me because otherwise, that would just be . . . disastrous.

Interview with a Pharmacist

ARI ROTH

A room in the Thunderbird Motel. JERRY talks straight ahead, as if addressing a video camera. In truth, he's being interviewed, by a student; a female undergraduate working her way through school. This is a part of her end-of-semester project, "Interviewing Tricks."

JERRY: Well, the name's Jerry. I own a chain of pharmacies. Two in Toledo. Four in Flint. Pretty good business. Or they *were*. Now every Meijer's 'n Kroger's got their own. Hard for the little guy. So I'm commuting now 'tween the different sites. We're open 'till 10 now, see. Keep up with the 24/7s. Which I can't. Wouldn't be any 'a me left if I did. But I try. Even if it means slashing profit. Good thing I don't have shareholders! I'd be dead! It's my wife's dad's store, see. He was against the expansion. But I had a dream. More like a nightmare. Then he died. So she blames me.

Otherwise, she's a good person. We're on different schedules, that's all. She's got the baby in bed by 9. Usually konks out with her. And I don't get in 'till after midnight, like I was saying. So relations are . . . you could say, sporadic. At best. If at all. Not that we don't want to. It's just . . . y'know . . . Hard. 'Cause she works too. And I love her working. Makes it easier for the both of us. To not be quite so resentful. Of missing out. That can happen in a marriage. People feel that they're missing. Even with all they have. I guess that's why I'm here.

'Cause I could do this to myself. I usually do. It's just I don't like myself so much when that happens. And it happens . . . a lot. And it's not even real. And you are. And I don't wanna hurt her. It's just . . . I don't want to have this kind of shame in my life anymore.

See, sometimes I'll come home; house'll be asleep. I'll make a bowl of cherry ice cream. Open the paper. Check for our display in the pull-outs. Make sure there've been no break-ins on the block. And right before I go up, I'll turn on the cable. Just for a second—See what I'm missing. I'll stare at the preview menu. The Pay-per-View trailers. And contemplate. How many can I get away with before she starts to notice? I make sure I always get the Paragon bill first. But what if I'm not home? Or out of town? And she opens the invoice before me and sees *Hot-Body Bikini*? *Luke's Peep Show*? So I just watch the promos. Every half-hour, a new set. But then I start feeling like some kinda pussy! What's stopping me? A man can't be expected to relinquish every last trace of desire!

I call the number. Got it memorized. Speed through the options. It's two in the morning. By 2:10, I hate myself. And the underwear is soaking wet. By 2:30, I'm at it again. Sort of a personal challenge. Because me and the wife, like I said, we don't usually . . . Never did. By 2:40, I shut the damn thing off. 2:50, it's back on again. I decide this has got to stop! What I'm doing; it's not even real! These girls—Their tits aren't real! Their lips aren't real! It's like that movie *Show-Girls*—Just a bunch'a plastic tramps, and some movie company makin' off with my money!

That's why I come to you, I guess. For a taste of the real. That's why most men come, isn't it? All I know is, I don't hate myself so much when I'm with you. Actually, I think I might even be, don't laugh, but . . . in love with . . . Hey, I thought I asked you not to laugh!

sweet dream

HARESH SHARMA

I guess it doesn't matter whether I'm dead or alive, happy or sad. I'll wake up anyway. Or maybe I won't.

My sister told me last night that when I was young, I died. Or so the doctor thought. And she swore she saw me leave my body.

I had fever. High fever. I was about 10. It was near the exams and I suppose I was worried. You see I had always been the best student, the top student, in school. But that year, there was a foreign student, Jacob, from Indonesia. He started getting better marks than me after the June holidays. So September came, and . . .

I could feel the fever coming. But I continued studying. It was only a week or so later, when my mother tried to wake me up that she realized how warm my body was. I remember mumbling something about having to go to school because the teacher was going to give some pointers about the exams. And I knew Jacob would be there listening to every word.

Jacob. Jacob Suyanto was a very handsome boy. I think I loved him. Once in a while when I'm watching TV, I think about him . . . wondering where he is. Whether he's fat. Whether he thinks of me when he's watching TV, wherever he is. Sometimes I wonder if he's still alive. I don't think he is. Well, he's not to me. My memories of him are like those of a person who's died. You remember certain images, you remember his face from a certain moment in time, and not even his whole face, but angels. Angels. He was an angel.

I died, for a few minutes, according to my sister. "I saw

you leave your body," that's what she said to me one day when we went out drinking with her boyfriend. She got really drunk. "I saw you leave your body." "Did I come back?" She laughed. Then her boyfriend laughed. I wasn't drinking. So I didn't find the humor in my question.

When I watch TV, and when I'm not thinking about Jacob, I think about the day I died. I don't remember bright lights or dead relatives with open arms. No voices, no angels, nothing. I was cold, shivering. There was a ringing in my ears. There was a tune which I couldn't quite make out. Maybe it was a tune I dreamt. I imagined.

I never told anyone this. But I always felt that after I came back from the hospital I was with a different family. But I could never quite explain why.

This is what I think happened. I died. I left my body. I went back into another body and came back to life. Which means that I'm really dead. The me that had a high fever and was shaking violently on the hospital bed. That died. That me probably got buried somewhere. But, I'm sure you're asking, if my sister saw me leave my body, and saw me come back to life, then I couldn't have died.

True.

Unless. Unless my body came back to life without me. So, what happened to me? Am I now here me? Or am I now here my body? If I'm my body, then where did I go? Where would a ten-year-old me, who had an exam in two weeks, go?

I believe I went to visit Jacob. I believe I sat by him as I watched him study. I believe I slept by his side, as he slept. I believe I am still with him. Wherever he is. Wherever I am.

I realize it doesn't matter whether I'm dead or alive. Happy or sad. I used to wonder why I was always depressed. After the fever, I wasn't as interested in school. Life just went along, with or without me. Time will not stop because of me. Day, night, month, year . . . they just go on whether you want them to or not. Your depression will not outlast the universe.

I didn't sleep last night. My sister stayed over at her

boyfriend's place. I came home. I had a shower in the dark. I wanted to feel my body as I soaped and scrubbed. I toweled myself and walked to my bedroom without the lights on. I lay in bed without any clothes on. Still in the dark.

I thought about what my sister said, "I saw you leave your body." And I was glad. I was glad she told me about my death. Coz suddenly I felt alive. Maybe because finally, finally I know that I am.

And I couldn't sleep last night because as I lay in bed, without my clothes, without the lights, I felt . . . for the first time, I believe I felt someone by my side.

The Pain of Passion

MATS HELLERSTEDT-THORIN

TOM BERNOWSKIJ, a middle-aged man, quite ordinary looking, is standing bent over a chair. He is in great pain.

TOM: Oh my God!!!! Ahhww! Shit! Breathe! Breathe! Breathe! Come on! BREATHE! (*Tries a few deep breaths.*) It's all right. No cause for alarm! I'm just in love! Bloody hell! I'm cracking up. Try not to think of her. Think of something else. I'm thinking of . . . thinking of . . . of . . . of . . . HER! Ahhhhhhhhhhhh!!!!! It's no good. (*Pause.*) If you think it's painful to be in love when you are a teenager you should try being in love at forty-four.

It started four months ago. I met my high school sweetheart for the first time in twenty-five years. She was in town and we just met up to talk about old times. We had a great time reminiscing and talking about what had happened the last twenty-five years. The next morning we had breakfast together. I don't know what happened but suddenly I found myself saying: "Breaking up from you all those years ago is number one on Tom Bernowskij's list of stupid mistakes. Please forgive me!"

Karen forgave me. We had a good cry. I took her to the train station. We said goodbye and what fun to see each other again.

I went home with a curious feeling of relief. Why? Had I had a guilty conscience all that time? I didn't think more about it, but two days later she called me just to say hello and thank you. We had a friendly chat. We hung up. I went to my old photo album and found old photos of us together when we were eighteen. I took the album to the toilet and sat down and cried for a good half hour.

Oh the pain! Sorry folks it's starting again. It's tough to suddenly be vulnerable again after so many years of being a good boy, bottling up so many feelings.

I emailed her and described my symptoms. She wrote back saying that she was experiencing the same sensations. I wrote to her again saying that my body is telling me to sort out my life and find my true priorities.

I realized I had lived for so many years taking care of others totally forgetting myself and my needs. I did nothing for days, not trying to find any answers, I just waited for the answers to find me. And suddenly one night I woke up and everything was clear. My body told me to get out of my marriage, which had been emotionally dead for years, and find out what my feelings for Karen were.

I broke the news to my wife who took it remarkably well and we decided together to get divorced. So here I am living in two parallel realities. In one I'm divorcing, dealing with practicalities like who should have what paintings and cutlery, and in one I'm madly, passionately in love completely consumed with this woman. I now realize I've missed her for twenty-five years. That is a lot of missing!

Living in two parallel worlds I tell you is not an easy thing.

Sorry! Stomach cramps again! Why the pain? Well, I guess I'm being reborn and giving birth is painful. Ask any woman. Usually giving birth doesn't take four months but this baby is being born slowly but surely. The new Tom Bernowskij is coming out and it's wonderful and so frightening.

Losing the emotional armour that I have carefully built to survive is like ripping band-aids from a very hairy chest, and it goes on and on and on. I'm exhausted!

Three months before we met again Karen cleaned her attic. From a cardboard box a letter fell out. She picked it up and read it. Guess what? It was a love letter I wrote to her when I was eighteen saying that I would never leave her. Well I kept my promise but it took me twenty-five years. Is that slow or is that slow?

Do I believe in premonitions? I didn't use to. I do now. Oh boy! Do I believe? Yes I believe!

I can just say: "Thank you whoever pulled the strings somewhere so that we found each other again! Thank you for giving me my life back again!"

(*Exits singing "I'm not in love!" by 10cc.*)

Grand People

MICHAEL YERGIN

MAN: Pretty nice house, ah, what'd I tell you? In this neighborhood? If you saw the people who live in there, you might think they were nuts. Not so, my friend. They've got a few secrets and tricks up their sleeves. They've got their daughter, Annie—a prize of the block and of the century of the block.

I've been in there, you know. I've been a friend. We've hobnobbed together over unpopular imported beers, her father and me. We have the same politics. I've painted that porch with Annie and her mother—a regular occurrence—and sat there in sun or rain drinking bitter homemade lemonade.

She might have her window open on a night like this, so just use your better judgment, if you don't mind. It's not that I think I'm out of line standing here this way. I mean she doesn't even know I'm here, that's not the point; if she knew, that's another thing, but she doesn't know because what the fuck, I'm whispering here, aren't I? And thank you for being quiet. Other guys might try to screw around. They might not respect the gravity of this thing.

And it's cold. I know. We'll go in a minute.

It's all about appearances, is the thing. You see the light up there: that's her. I mean I'm not sure but I'm betting. No one else uses the attic. I just wish she were standing. You could see how she's shaped.

The light in that attic there, it's this funny contraption, turned on with a red strand of yarn that hangs down from the ceiling. It's about this long and as thick as that hose lying there in the flowers. Don't ask me who rigged it up, maybe the whole family sat to dinner and rigged it up together, that's the way they are, at least that's what I saw when I was thought hip enough to be invited inside. They found out I wasn't so hip after all when Annie came home one night, in a certain state and when I—I'll tell you they have rough pasts, her folks. That's why they're such purists. I think I must have seemed new once, and I was loved for it. It was when I became reminiscent that it was over.

But I've been inside of that attic. I've seen that light rig up close.

Annie, she'd be all right with a visit from me. It's just her folks, really. Not that they're assholes. They're grand people. She's young, they've got valid concerns, I share them, they just don't know I share them is the thing. I share them more than the people they think share them, if you actually look at it.

I bet you, and I'm just saying, I bet you that if I could get her to notice me down here she would sneak me in. Play one of her records for me. And, of course, ask me for a cigarette. We got started on the same night. I'd have to be confident, if I didn't want her to ruin the whole thing by crying. But I would be. I'd be confident and strong and I'd hold her if she wanted or I'd just show her I had put myself back together. And I'm not saying sex, if that's what you're thinking. I'm saying communion. Redemption, like.

I'd say "Annie, I know you're on the right track, so am I see, I am too, and we could be together, we could kick ass together and knock away all the smirking faces together, all the—and we'd be laughing last, Annie. We'd be happy." We'd take long walks at night and reveal our secret identities to one another. It'd be a life like our grandparents had. And nobody would remember.

Do you think I could throw a stone at her window, or a penny or something? Here, I'll throw my cigarette box. . . . Fuck, man, it's stuck! It's stuck on the fucking ledge.

Come over here. No, over here. Please. Thank you. I'm sorry. Just wait here a minute. I'm just going to check that window again. I just have an odd feeling. (*Quiet, a warm-up, looking down.*) Annie . . . Annie . . . Annie . . . (*Speaking voice, looking up.*) Annie. (*A breath, and then, three times quickly, Stanley/Stella/Jungle style.*) ANNIE! ANNIE! ANNIE! (*Turns.*) Fuck! Go!

    (*He does a full circle, as slow-motion discus thrower. At 180 degrees he is poised to run, at 360, he is still and unafraid.*)

    No. Wait.

The World We Knew Under Siege

S HATTERED. I'VE BEEN BLASTED WIDE OPEN. But, wait! I want my innocence back. I want my eating-Campbell's-Chicken-Noodle-Soup, watching-*I-Love-Lucy*-re-reruns, wondering-why-Debbie-Hall-isn't-wearing-my-i.d.-bracelet-to-school innocence back. I don't want to think about terrorists and planes crashing into buildings and grey dust in my air and down my lungs and in my soul and burrowing deep into my already-darkened heart. I WANT MY BLUE SKY BACK. I WASN'T READY . . . Exactly—your point, I believe.

I was still worried about the rubber trees being cut down in different parts of the world and whether my Rav-4 is rolling around Manhattan on four Crimes of Nature. I was stressing over a fucked up ecosystem that's on a self-timer, and whether I should be using aluminum foil or spray deodorant because it can cause Alzheimer's, and Mexican nationals that boxed themselves up with a dream of freedom, but delivered themselves dead in a train to my America.

I was still sorting out whether I should hold a door open for ANYONE—man, woman, dog, or goat—because I think it's a polite thing to do but the woman will just think I'm hitting on her, the guy will just think I'm hitting on him, the dog won't trust my intentions, and the goat's just stupid and doesn't count anyway.

I was still focused on whether I should be taking an aspirin a day, and the Nazi war criminals on trial for atrocities to the heart of mankind, and whether AIDS was making a comeback to a disco beat, and why whales were sunning themselves permanently on the beaches of Florida . . . and . . . YOU'VE FUCKIN' INTERRUPTED MY FLOW, MAN,

MY SPIRALING NEUROSIS, MY MUSHROOMING ITCH! YOU RUINED IT FOR ME!

You've made me care that you really exist in the world, instead of just ignoring you in the *New York Times*. You've made me question God and safety and trust and mankind and . . . You selfish fucks! You forced me to consider you. You forced me to care that you exist. You forced me to stare coldly into my future. You've rattled me. You've shaken my core. And I will never, ever be the same . . .

BUT! You didn't win, mother fucker. Ohhhhhhhhhh, no. You'll have to work a lot harder than that because I have this spirit in me that's impenetrable. Test me again, bitch. Slap at me and watch as I break your hand, bone by bone.

Dreaming Angel

PAUL AUSTIN

HARVEY: I woke up this morning lying in bed thinking I am you lying in bed thinking about me. Honest to God, I'm not thinking *about* you, I *am* you. And you're thinking about me. I mean, I couldn't say *what* you were thinking, but I can *feel* myself *feel* you thinking about me. It's not specific thoughts because it's not me anymore, it's you. Well, biologically it's still me, naturally, but it's not me, the inner me. The inner me isn't anymore. The inner me is actually you. But I couldn't prove it to you—that my actual biological self has become somebody else—I just *know* it's you. Don't say anything, okay?

Then I realize what I'm doing, which means I guess, that I'm me again. Then I start to miss you. As if you'd actually been there and you'd left. At first, it's like you just left, but after a few seconds it's like you've been away a long time. Then I get this crazy thought that if I can imagine I'm you again, you won't go away. But I can't. And I'm thinking, "Okay, I can't make this happen, it has to happen by itself." I mean, I'm not calling to ask you necessarily to stick around all the time. I'm just saying that's what was happening this morning, okay?

So then I turned on the radio and I hear that another suicide bomber has blown himself up and sixteen other people with him. Some children too. So now I'm thinking. "Shit, this is never going to end, is it? The killing, the torture, the starvation. In Sudan, the Philippines, Guatemala, wherever. It's all just going to go on, isn't it?" I mean, it's *me* thinking—not you, not somebody—it's *me*, myself, that is doing the thinking. It's going to go on and on, is what I'm thinking, all the killing and cruelty is just going to continue like no individual life ever mattered.

The thing is, I thought that 9/11 ended something. I thought, *me* thinking, I thought it was so big, it was such a catastrophe, that everybody—who is everybody? I don't know. I guess I thought the whole world would catch on. You know, we'd crossed a line, this would be it. We'll all quit this now. But it didn't make any difference, did it? Americans think it's different, but it's not. It's just the same old, same old.

The radio people were still talking in that too-fast way they do, that no matter what happens they have to say it fast to make room for the commercial. It's a girl, I hear, a young girl. Who is she? I wonder, the suicide bomber. I imagine she's pretty. Guys do that, I guess, imagine all young girls are pretty. Why would she do that? I'm thinking. And then I'm trembling because—honest to God—I can feel myself walking on the bus. There's a lot of people on the bus—that's good—because I'm supposed to blow up as many people as I can. People are doing things with their bodies and their mouths, with each other and themselves, but they're only forms. I don't hear anything, I only see these hot, shimmering, vibrating forms. Everything is bright, bright and white like gold, bright, white gold. And hot. The whole bus is steaming and shimmering and vibrating. I feel the sweat searing my eyes. I can feel the bomb strapped around me, and I can feel it ticking. And my heart is ticking just like it and I'm wondering—it's *me* now, back on my bed—and I'm wondering if I'm going to have a heart attack, if my biological self is going to explode.

Then I was remembering an old-timey song that used to be one of my parents' favorites—*All I do is dream of you, dream of you the whole day through*. And I'm wondering do you dream of me? Does Angel dream of me? But how could she dream of me, I'm thinking. I don't dream of her, do I? I dream I *am* her. Who am I then who can't dream *of* somebody? People call me Harvey. But am I? I mean, was I ever really all that hot for Popeye's chicken? Somebody used to know how many freckles you had on the small of your back. Who was that? I mean, what do you do when all concept of yourself becomes unimportant, when all references to self become absurd. What do you do when there's no *me*? Don't hang up, okay? Because this is why I called.

See, I realized that all this happened after you left. No, listen, I'm not asking when you're coming back. I just . . . well, would you do me a favor? Don't answer, okay? You'll do it or you won't, that's all. Would you write me a note? Send it to *Harvey White*. You know the address. All you have to say is "Hello, Harvey." Not just "hello" though. Be sure you say my name. "Hello, Harvey." You can write other stuff, if you want. You know, how you're doing, if you're working, stuff like that. You don't have to though. All you have to write is 'Hello, Harvey.' All you have to do is say my name, okay? Okay, that's it, Angel, that's all I wanted to say. 'Bye. I'll wait till you hang up. 'Bye.

Whalespeak

AARON CABELL

A concerned citizen at night court.

CITIZEN: Your Honor, this whole thing looks a little crazy, I know. I'm willing to take my punishment, pay the fine, do the time, whatever. Dumping a barrel of fish guts in the lobby of the EPA is drastic, I admit . . . but I had to be heard. It was a smelly, disgusting act, I admit, but people have to know the truth I know. I tried to go through channels. I wrote, emailed, called. Nobody would listen. Even Greenpeace wouldn't see me. It all started on TV.

I was watching and eating a tuna-fish sandwich and saw a news report where something like forty whales beached themselves, on the same beach, all at once. If you're like me, I'm sure you've been amazed by this curious phenomenon. It's not the first time this has happened either. We arrogantly try to explain it in various ways: "They got lost," their internal sonar or whatever has "failed." . . . I heard one guy blame it on solar flares . . . whatever. Every explanation we come up with keeps us at the top of the food chain, intelligence-wise.

Lookit. Forty whales. One beach. All at once. Something's goin' on. Amazing pictures. Aerial shots of people swarming the whales like ants. Concerned citizens gettin' busy, takin' action, tryin' to do the right thing . . . Save the Whales! But they were missing the point. While waiting for the tide to come in, these people stayed up all night keeping the whales wet and protecting them from sunburn—but they didn't get it. The citizens worked tirelessly and saved all but nine or ten. When the water was deep enough, they pushed the whales back into the safety of the ocean. The very next morning, the motherfuckahs came back! S'cuse my language, your honor, but I get excited every time I think about it. Something's goin' on. What would possess them to ignore every survival instinct? Sun spots? I don't think so. . . . Then Bam! I dropped the sandwich! I figured it out! It came to me . . . clear, crystal . . . like a shot! Don't you see? It was a mass suicide as political protest.

Wait, wait, wait, just hear me out your honor. Lookit. Our species does the same thing every day. It's all through history. Teenagers strapping C-4 to themselves on crowded buses in Tel Aviv. Remember those Buddhist monks who set themselves on fire to protest the Vietnam War? The Jews of Masada really freaked the Romans out. I wonder how many times a beached whale has coincided with something terrible happening among humans? Somebody should do a study and look for connections between terrestrial and aquatic events.

I'm telling ya, something's goin' on.

Let's stop patronizing the whales. Let's give 'em some credit. We all agree that they're highly intelligent with brains as sophisticated as our own. We know that they have a very complicated social structure and have been here, on this planet, unchanged, for a helluva lot longer than we have. We need to face the possibility that they're actually trying to tell us something. What if they're saying: "Hey you assholes, stop over-fishing and pissing in our water." S'cuse me your honor, but they're saying "How would you like it if we dumped all our shit where you live?"

Now I don't know why I was chosen to see this. It just hit me that, because of us, the ocean has become so fuc– I mean, messed up that it ain't habitable for them. Maybe the water tastes and feels sooo bad that it just ain't worth existing in anymore. Maybe the protest is as simple as that . . . since we're polluting their environment, they choose to return the favor by using their own bodies as garbage in ours.

I was in Florida a few years back when a Sperm whale beached herself. She was pregnant. It took a week to cut the thing up and clear the beach. What would possess a mother to ignore every survival instinct? Your honor, don't ya' get it? It was Election Day 2000. The stench was unbelievable.

Darren

CHRIS DUNKLEY

He wears a knitted woollen hat with a woollen ball, a bobble, attached to the crown.

I figured out the hat situation
There's a lot of money on doorsteps don't pretend you're not
listenin' this could make us if
you want it
So i figured out the HATS if you'd be so kind
Just remember snow baseball cap, rain no hat at all, autumn
beret and the rest of the time
bobblehat
You got a bobblehat?
Fuckin' get one
Otherwise you won't make jack shit
If it rains in the autumn, you gotta use your judgement

Look 'em in the eye offer the goods but make sure they notice
the hat
I'm tryin' at least

At least i'm tryin'

An flick 'em the ole smile

Let 'em fink they can't fuck you

For a bloke you give it some right mean smile like i'm gonna
rip you off y'bastard but he's
thinkin' you ain't gonna rip ME off son 'cos i'm too fuckin'
clever for the likes o' you, you piece of shit

An' never ever let 'em arsk you why

Cos when they arsk you why, they got you

No duckin', no dodgin' it

If they arsk iss cos' they wanna know

Why

Why wot

Why you doin' community

Community service

Community service you fuckin' drone

Why

Wha' did you do to make them make you do community fuckin' service

Cos then they got you then see

'Specially the women

why, they say and theywon'teverletitgo, why the women say armsfolded undertheirtits like they're gonna drop off an' they never letitgo

the truth is under my hat

an' anyway it ain't community service

i'm sellin' this shit on your doorstep 'cos i ain't got no uvver choice

'cours i 'AVE got a choice but it ain't no fuckin' choice no
fuckin' choice at all not a choice a choice that 'cos y'see i
started readin' inside
i started readin' inside
but no fucker thought i was actually readin' it

all thought i was tryin' t'get early release on the grounds of i
dunnowhat good behaviour i s'pose but good behaviour really
depends on wha' you read
they shoulda kept me in for bad behaviour the shit i was
readin'

so why you doin' community

see they never let it go
they never fuckin' let it go
well it gets to a certain point an' there's no avoidin' it
you gotta say
you gotta tell

an' i shift my hat

i was expelled
from school
kicked out
because
'cos
just 'cos

an' there's a look of relief on their face

only expelled from school

yeah but i went back up there

wiv a gun

a gun

a gun

wiv a gun

see

they never listened to me

an' the teacher didn't make sense to me

never a word of fuckin' sense

I
Never
Knew
What
They
Wanted
From
Me

The bitch weren't makin' no sense

'Course they reckon i might be a little bit deaf
thass what they reckon
thass what they figure
what they fink
now
only now

i found 'er
found 'er sittin' in a toilet

hidin'

from me

an' i could hear the gun go off

heard that much

not so deaf now

'course, they got you

once they arsk why

an' you shift your hat

an' you tell 'em

then the door closes

The Exhibit

BEN ELLIS

ADRIAN, in his mid-30s, sits on a chair. He makes a face to some-one else as if to ask, "Is it my turn now?" He stands, clears his throat, looks around him, smirks, pulls a notebook out of his pants and begins.

ADRIAN: My name's Adrian. And I'm a male. I've struggled not to act like a male for the four days since they sent me to this group.

Sorry to the women here to make it sound like it's all Males Anonymous, but, according to Them, I've been indulging in . . . "inappropriate" masculinist behaviors at work. Hence this enforced appearance. I am required to "talk" through my "issues" before I can go back.

Before you dismiss me as a blokey "dinosaur," let me say this. In the modern workplace, men cannot afford to be wimps. We have to put our arguments as forcefully as we can. We're all under threat, and as a modern Student Welfare Coordinator, I especially cannot be seen to be weak. If two feminists in my workplace want to describe it as getting my dick out and bang-ing it on the table, let them go ahead and say it. It's not like they don't hide behind their gender. So I get my dick out and I bang it on the table. Figuratively, of course. (*Beat.*)

So you don't think I'm "old-fashioned," I would like to present to you this exhibit. This 48-page A5 exercise book is one of many, which my "partner" and I keep at home, our log of household duties. (*Hands the notebook to an audience mem-ber.*) Over the last three years, I have washed the dishes 62.3% of the time. I have done the vacuuming 97.5%—the only times I failed to do so being when I fell sick. And I love dusting. I love collecting dust, with a big blue fluffy duster, and then stepping back to see how much clearer the mantelpiece or the top of the TV is. I do 45.8% of the dusting. Not bad considering the total amount of housework I do. According to the Facts, in this—may I say meticulously kept—book, I have done almost half of the household duties.

From the studies I have read about what the average Australian male does around the home, I do ten times what he doesn't. So, I've built up some credits. I think I deserve pay-back for all I put in. Blonde jokes. Anna Kournikova screen-savers. That Australian Women's Soccer Calendar for 2000. That's right—the nudey one. Look at the book. I've even cooked.

I understand about the personal being political. Isn't it obvious? I'm the radical here. I've built up Equality-in-the-Home Feminist Credits. Why don't I deserve the occasional withdrawal, the odd debit? Isn't equality about finding the balance between the male and the female? For me, I find the balance in the workplace after doing my bit at home. They don't say it out loud, but those feminists are just attacking me for being a man. They don't like the fact that I've got a penis. If they want to criticize me for being a man, then I'm going to throw that manhood back in their face. Figuratively, of course.

Figuratively. It's not a "problem." It's a choice. Unlike the rest of you I don't have any "problems." So I got my dick out and banged it on the table. Literally. More than once. Quite a few times. But I made my point.

It's the pressures of the modern feminised workplace. And I'm not going to stand by and see it squash me. Not like you, Mr. Wants-to-Bash-Up-His-Chemistry-Supervisor-but-Has-Father-Issues. Wanker. You can laugh, Miss Turn-all-Power-Points-Off-Obsessive-Compulsive. I can see what your problem is—you're a stalker. Your friend's avoiding you, hanging out with her boyfriend for protection from your schoolgirl lesbian crush. The fact that you're fifty-eight years old only makes it more disgusting.

And as for you, I don't see at all how this talking is helping anybody work through their so-called problems. I think the real problem is that you want to make all of our innate male eccentricities "problems" . . . (*Pause.*) I'm sorry. But I really, really want to get my dick out now. Do you mind?

Prenatal Paralysis

DAVID FRANK

Okay, you're anxious, of course you are—you can't always know the right thing to do. So you buy the gas masks, you buy the chemical suits for you and Susie and the kids, you get a car and you plan the best escape route in the event of some new attack. And you buy a month's supply of storable food and pray you never have to use it. And, of course, you consider moving the hell out of the city altogether!

But listen Paul, at least you have your kids. We were moving further downtown so we could start our family. And then, when the towers fell, we were like "What the fuck are we doing, we just moved closer to Wall Street?!"

But Denise and I had talked about it a lot and decided that we really did want children, in spite of everything that had happened. And it was time to start trying. Now you know how fucked up my life has been lately. I was fully prepared for this process to take forever because nothing ever comes easy. Then I started getting anxious and having trouble sleeping and things didn't seem so clear anymore. But I kept quiet and on a Monday night in February we finally pulled the goalie. We made love almost every night that week, trying to increase our chances. After each climax, I grabbed Denise's ankles and held them up over my head. I wanted to make damn sure all my soldiers of fortune were headed in the right direction. On Saturday night at about 4:00 A.M., having just finished the deed, I stumbled into the bathroom. That was when I first noticed I had blood on me. Now we'd had a little spotting at other times, but this was different. I looked at Denise. She was bleeding. Parts of her lower half were covered in blood. The sheets and the bed were bloody. We panicked. We didn't know what was happening or what to do. We thought about rushing her to the emergency room. But we just sat there and cried. Finally the bleeding stopped. I figured if Denise had gotten pregnant that first week, then she had just miscarried.

And then I really started to wonder. I thought maybe it was for the best. Maybe we shouldn't be bringing a child into a world this fucked up; where hostile cultures can erase thousands of us with one horrible act; where we have enemies all over the planet who love to hate us and half the time we deserve it; where in my own neighborhood last month, one block from my new apartment, three people were murdered in their beds by a very disturbed teenager who then did horrible things to the dead bodies. Is it fair to bring a child into all this? Can we, as parents, offer any real security or answer any of the big questions with a sense of honesty or true understanding? I have no fucking idea. But then I got really scared. The thought struck me that maybe we wouldn't be able to conceive at all. After all that soul searching and waiting for the right time and preparing a nice home, maybe after all that, the decision would be made for us: We can't get pregnant, we're not going to be parents. That's heartbreaking to me, Paul. I can't picture my life without more family in it. I don't want to miss the chance to be a father. Now I don't know what to do. And I don't know if there's anything I can do . . .

So we're just waiting for our gynecologist appointment to see what's going on with Denise.

I know you're probably right. But it's easy for you to say: you've got two healthy boys who idolize you. So what if you live in the number one terrorist target in the world! You've been blessed, Paul. I don't know what's going to happen to us.

Barry, the Human Sponge

GRAHAM GORDY

BARRY, early 30's, rushes up. He starts out fast and just gets faster. He's on a mission.

BARRY: Honey, we are leaving *right now*, do you understand me? And I'm not taking "no" for an answer and I don't care how many more things you need to get 'cause our days here are over. *(Trying to catch his breath.)*

I'm freakin' out here. I can't . . . breathe. I can't catch my breath. Jesus Christ, it's the same thing that happened when we visited Times Square and I ended up curled up in a ball on the sidewalk. *(Fanning himself.)* It's like there's so much stimuli and I have no . . . filtration. I don't filter. I can't filter things out, ya' know? I gotta sit down. I gotta get a chair. Where's *Lawn and Garden*?

. . . Are you . . . ? Is that a laugh? Are you laughing at this? This is *just* like you, I swear. This could be a condition. A real illness this time, but not to you. No. Not a hand to be offered. They're all filled with teeth whiteners and vaginal creams . . . I'm so confused. WHATTA THEY WANT YOU TO LOOK AT IN THIS PLACE?! *(He sits on the floor.)*

You don't believe me? Right here. Right now. Sight. Without even moving. White Keds, double-knotted. Legs. Yours. Well-tanned in exposed areas. Shorts. Khaki. Pleated. Gap, no doubt. Seeming acres of cheap ceramic tile. Aisles, blessed aisles of *hair products*. Ahhh. Mango/Kiwi Madness. Lavender and Jojoba. Papaya/Eucalyptus/Passion Fruit. Peripheral, I got Coconut, Calendula, and Oatmeal. Are they hair colors, hairstyles, or hair flavors? Nobody knows, but we all care. So many colors and smells vying for my attention, who could refuse? And me, I'm a human sponge, honey, *doomed* to take it all in. (*He gets up. In her face.*)

And we haven't even gotten to the meanings. A world without meaning? Oh no. Imbued with it. Nothing but meaning here. All meaning, any meaning. As long as it's not a deep meaning, that slows us down. (*He hands her bottles.*) This will make me salon beautiful. This will make me tingle. And this will BRING ME TO ORGASM!

And I can't distinguish anymore, honey. That's the thing. My brain no longer distinguishes important information from unimportant. I can tell you how many CC's the new Honda Shadow has, but I can't remember my own mother's birthday. What is real? What's fake? I was just in the magazine aisle and I swear the woman on the cover of *Good Housekeeping* was coming on to me.

. . . How much can a single consciousness take? I'm at my limit, baby. C'mon. I wanna get out of Wal-Mart.

Just Do It

ADRIAN PAGE

Cacophony of media sound bites. Spotlight up. A MAN sits. A TV flickers on his face.

MAN: And suddenly it stopped. And all around the sky went black. The blast lasted seconds. Newspapers crumpled. I felt something. Once. I thought. I saw it on TV. Technicolor. My brothers burning. The world stopped turning. I saw it on TV. In the shop. I was shopping. Hoping to pick up a new TV. I shop a lot. Like that. The screens surrounded me. Screaming at me. Adverts sadverts adverts madverts. Flicker. Lights out. Flicker. Smoke rose. Flicker. Walls closed in on me. Surround sound surrounded me. I dropped my Sainsbury's bag. In shock. Fresh fruit fell. Modified mangoes melt on metal glass. TV screen screamed. Smoke. Flash. News. Views. The queue at the counter counteracted my conflicting emotions. Should I go JVC. Or Sony? Questions. Questions. An old woman fell. Fainted. Tainted glass caught her gaze. Newscaster wept. I waited for adverts. To tell me what to do. Just do it. Said one. I'd learnt it by heart. Just do it. Just do it. *JUST DO WHAT!?* Nothing. Said the store detective. Do nothing. Should I pay by cheque. Or card? I have no cash. These days. These plastic days. Smoke spilt. Could smell it. Never seen a plane potentially penetrate the Pentagon. Hexagonal pixels pixilated. My face fixated. The newscaster. Broke. News. Spoke in tongues. I felt. Once. I saw it on TV. I had enough for a Panasonic. Sonic boom of a supersonic 747. Or was it another? Never was a plane spotter. TV screamed. A crowd converged. Felt fifty-five channels fluctuate. The old lady lay on the concrete. Oblivious to world destruction. Crowd converged. Market stood still. Static. Freeze frame. Does this have remote control? I enquire. Everything you want and more. Store detective spoke. A hushed tone. I just want a TV. I just want a DVD. I just want a JVC TV and DVD. No DVD for me. Had everyone taken leave of their senses? Or was it me? I'll go JVC crazy if they let me. I've saved for years for this moment. News. Flash. Interrupting all broadcasts. To bring a message. The world . . . was no longer . . . safe. What's new? What's news? Where's the drama in that? Seen it a billion times on big screens. Jumbo jets on TV sets don't scare me. It dawned on me. The newscaster swooned. Her face red. Smoke spilled. World went wild. Store stood still—silent. The woman on the pavement spasmed like a spastic. But I need a TV. If only she knew. How much I need that screen. There were gasps. Gosh. God. God? God. Lots of Gods' names were proclaimed. I heard them all. But knew none of them. A child cried. She couldn't have a Big Mac. But the world is blowing up. Her mother declared with disdain. I don't fucking care. I want a TV. And she wants a Big Mac. I knew how she felt. I felt her pain. Women in yashmaks hid in the streets. And any urbanite in a turban had better beware. Old lady's heart pounded. Bereft of breath. I had to sit down soon. No room on the shop floor. Crowd swelled. Till beeped. Electric eye swept shop floor. I paid good money for those mangoes. Exotic fruit is hard to find on the open market. I was lucky. Child was not happy. Old lady melted into the tarmacadam. Can I get Sky? Satellite? Sports channel? All of these and more. Store detective's eyes said it all. He knew not what he was protecting anymore. Breaking. News. You can get it twenty-four-seven now. Detective said knowingly. He'd learnt his lesson the hard way. Stunned. I think is the word. Stunned with an infrared zapper. The channel won't change. I protested. It's all the same. Every channel. Same. Blast. Smoke. Scream. Flash. News. Broken. Shattered.

Look Before You Leap

MOSHE KASHER

I guess I really thought that it was over. (*Pause.*)
Fucking stupid.
I thought . . . this is San Francisco . . . ground zero . . .
It's 2002.
This is where safe sex was invented.
Nobody gets HIV anymore.
Fucking stupid. (*Pause.*)
My . . . my . . . my . . . t-cells are dropping they said.
I cannot even fucking believe this.
I haven't even come out.
I'm not even fucking gay yet and I'm dying.
I'm dying. (*Pause.*)
Well I'm not sick yet but it's just a matter of time.
I am going to die.
From this . . . thing. (*Pause.*)
Now what do I do?
What do I tell my parents?
Kill two birds with one stone.
Mom . . . Dad . . .You know how you told me you would love
me no matter what . . . That I was your son and that family
means everything and that I should never be afraid to tell you
anything and that you weren't just my parents but you were
my friends too and that I was your perfect little angel and that
you would love me forever and ever and ever. . . . Remember
that? (*Pause.*) Yes? Good . . .
Well . . . I'm gay . . .
I fuck guys. Good. Is that all in order? . . . Tears? . . .Yes.

(*Agreement.*)

Yes! (*Shocked.*) . . . I will (*Placating.*) . . .Yes. (*Understanding.*)

Great . . .

I'm gay!

You love me anyway?

Terrific!

Oh yes . . . also . . .

I'm dying.

I've got AIDS and I'm dying.

Hmm! Yes . . .

I am going to die.

Your perfect little angel.

He got fucked up the ass by some Latin daddy at the bath-house and now?

He's dying.

Shame.

Yeah, well anyway sorry to have kept it from you and all that . . . Love you too . . . please send money. . . . See you when I'm in the hospital, breathing with a machine! OK love you too mom . . .

Love you too. (*Pause.*)

And then you got these "old guard" 50-year-old queens telling you how lucky you are to have gotten it now.

How it's not a death sentence anymore.

New procedures . . .

New treatments . . .

Plenty of exercise . . .

Eat healthy . . .

Fuck you!

Fuck you.

It doesn't feel like a lucky time to get AIDS.

Feels like shit.

And no I don't care that you lost your partner in the 80's and no I don't care about how destroyed you were and no I don't care how it made you fight to eradicate it from the world. Because . . .

It didn't work.

IT'S TEN YEARS LATER AND I'M FUCKING DYING BECAUSE YOU DIDN'T TELL HECTOR YOUR SAD LITTLE STORY!!

Hector didn't care!

Hector just wanted to bust a nut in some little skinny white boy who just couldn't say . . . Stop.

Do you have a condom?

Could you wear a condom?

No that would have fucked up the game.

Yes sir . . .

No sir . . .

Yes I am a little faggot . . .

Yes I do want to get fucked . . . (*Switch*.)

Wait a minute . . . Do you have a rubber?

I won't lay down for this!

This is serious! (*Pause*.)

And it fucking felt great.

I never even thought.

He was so big and healthy looking.

Six months later I stopped seeing him around.

I asked if anyone had seen him.

They said he went home to his mom's house to die.

TO DIE?!?!

HIS DICK WAS IN MY ASS!

I'M GOING TO DIE!

I'm going to die.

My dad used to say . . . "Son, someday you'll realize that life isn't fair.

Sometimes you just get what you get."

Thanks for the words of wisdom, Pop.

You were right.

I got it!

I got what I got!

Still wanna have those "man to mans?" (*Pause*.)

Someday there will be a picture of me on the mantel . . .

Or maybe there won't be a picture of me on the mantel.
And I'll be the dirty little secret
The thing not to bring up at Christmastime.
Just because mom's so sensitive about him.
Just don't mention his name . . .
She just gets so upset.
Since he . . .
You know . . .
It would just be better . . .
If you could . . .
Not . . .
Mention . . .
The faggot.
The dead faggot.

Rashid's Rant

BRAD ROTHBART

RASHID: Yo dogg, this hero shit is wack. No fireman, no
policeman's a fuckin' hero. They asked for this shit, they
trained for this shit, and they agreed to die for this shit. This
ain't Russia, they are not forced at age six to be rescue workers
for the glory of the country.

I'm not layin' down no dis, bro.—I give 'em mad props
for doin' that shit. They fuckin' braver than me. I hear the
deal—they got 'rents, rels, peeps who depend on their ass, and
now they gone tryin' to save somebody they don' even know.
It's sad, man, real fuckin' sad. But they knew the job when
they took it on. In my book, ain't nobody a hero for doin'
their fuckin' job. Mythos without Ethos equals Pathos. You
can go to school on that.

But that just the first muthafuckin' level. If people a hero
for doin' their jobs, if that all it takes, then everybody some
kinda hero. If everybody a hero, then nobody a hero, cause
bein' a hero mean doin' somethin' amazin', and if everybody
doin' it, who left to be the fuck amazed? You feelin' me? If we
go the other direction on this twisted-ass concept and say that
bein' a hero the GOAL, and almost nobody ever get to be
one—that means if you ain't a hero, you ain't shit. That what
King George II want, bro. People lot easier to control if they
think they ain't shit.

You realize we lost, right, dogg? We lost this war. We lost
when we didn't take enough time to mourn. We shoulda shut
down the country, held hands, cried together, buried the dead
we could find and thought for a good long time about how to

go forward. Fuckin' Texas macho shit got this country all screwed up, bro. The minute we attacked and killed even one innocent person, we became them. Hear that good. We became them. It ain't about terrorism, it about revenge. Ain't no stupid-ass, goofy Alfred E. Neuman-looking, hiding-in-Nebraska muthafucka gonna tell me different.

Now we losin' this war all over again. All this Homeland Security bullshit. King George II must think Americans are some kinda genius, or everybody else is a total fuckin' idiot. Check this: When they hit us, they did it by attacking in a way we never dreamed of. We had all these spies, all this fuckin' "intelligence," and we never saw it comin'. Now we busy announcin' how secure we are in every way. Does ol' King George II think they don't read newspapers or watch TV? They gonna do exactly what they did the first time, figure out what we ready for and do somethin' else. But that ain't even the worst part, dogg. I heard that in order to fund this stupid Homeland Security shit, ol' King George II is gonna end a program that gives free heat for old people. The way I figure it, if you old, poor and American, you can feel safe and secure as you freeze to death in you icy-ass apartment. They won the fuckin' war, bro. I tell you that straight up.

1 BR, Walk-In Kitchen

GARY SUNSHINE

ROGER, 27, speaks to his soon-to-be-ex-roommate, Maya.

ROGER: So I lied, Maya. The apartment I looked at on Thursday? It wasn't such a dump. A large person could live there. A large person who cohabitates with an even larger person, they could both live largely there.

I got to the building and the super told me it's 5L, rent-stabilized, and it's going for only eleven hundred, a real one bedroom, with a walk-in kitchen. So I want to kiss the super, but I restrain myself, because he has a smell that doesn't work for me. Then he says, it's still in litigation. Turns out 5L was occupied by the same guy for about fifteen years, until he died last month. "But don't worry," the super tells me, "he died in the hospital."

So we go up and the super unlocks the apartment and on the living room floor I immediately see a pile of newspapers with a roll of masking tape next to it. Packing material. Not the kind of stuff that says anything specific about a person. Which relieves me.

I turn around to the kitchen. It's clean and mostly bare. Except there are these two postcards taped to the refrigerator. One card's got a set of abs cut with a steak knife and ready to eat. The other's a picture of that woman from the forties I can't stand, what's her name? She looks like the Chiquita Banana commercial . . . not Rita Hayworth, not Lauren Bacall, she speaks with that really thick accent, with those painted eyebrows, everything's all about sex, what's her name . . . Lupe Miranda? Whatever. Her eyes follow me wherever I move.

I wander off to the bathroom, where there's soap in the soap dish. I peek in the medicine cabinet. I find a bottle of Obsession. So post-*Dynasty* pre-*Roseanne*, total time warp. (*Pulls out a bottle of Obsession and places it down.*)

Give it to your brother, he'll love it. I also see an eyelash curler. (*Pulls out the curler and places it down.*) For your faggy dad, with admiration.

Then I see maybe ten different prescriptions. I wondered if this is the cocktail. The protease stuff. I don't know what protease looks like. I didn't touch them. I wanted to see the guy's name, but it felt like too much of an invasion.

I finally get to the bedroom. You'd get a rash from the mess. Receipts and papers and junk all over the floor, not to mention about three thousand Judy Garland tapes and CDs. I still don't get her. A little rehab and a supportive recovery community and would anyone even remember her name today?

So there are all those tapes and CDs on the floor. Some porn, too, old Colt stuff. That's already in my sock drawer. I saw some books. Stonewall this. Stonewall that. And a high school yearbook with a big, gold 1975 on the cover. The year I was born. This guy was probably trying to get it up for his prom date while Rabbi Landsman was snipping at my down there with his penknife.

I thought about taking the yearbook, but by now, I was starting to get a little dizzy, my breathing wasn't working the way it should. I mean, here I am in this one-bedroom pit on a dig, and I keep tripping on one homo artifact after another, remnants of a dying generation of "pioneers." We're supposed to respect these guys and I guess mourn for them . . . but I just can't. So I want to fly from this pit, out the door and back to you, Maya. I just love you so fucking much, for whatever that's worth.

But I realize this is an air-conditioned, well-lit pit. A pit that will accommodate my glamorous futon, my maple-veneer chest of drawers, my shoe rack. A pit I could get lost in.

Only one question left . . . the closet. I slide open the closet doors, and inside it's as big as Alaska. Home free, right?

I turn to leave the bedroom, when my eye catches something. Sitting neatly in the corner of the closet . . . (*Pulls out an enormous brown fishing boot.*) The other one's still there. A hundred rubber trees died for these boots, I'm thinking. Fishing has nothing to do with Lupe Miranda or Judy Garland or Stonewall or protease inhibitors, I'm thinking. These boots don't fucking belong here.

I smelled each boot. I put my hands inside each boot. And I hoped the insides would be a little sweaty, or even fish-stenchy, from use. Just to feel this guy alive, even for a second. To see him as a person, no more. But the boots were dry. Dry and cold. And I couldn't smell a thing.

Re-Mirroring

I need a re-mirror. That's right. I need something else to come back in that reflection. God knows I try. I fill my head with all sorts of fancy, frilly delusions. But damned if it doesn't look like me every time I look. And that's not me, really. That's not my identity.

The real me is tall and muscular and manly and I've got these white teeth that George Hamilton would be proud to call his own. And I've got an intellect that Allan Greenspan would covet. And I've got a knowledge of world politics that little Georgey Bushy can only dream of having while sucking on his big thumb. And I can rap better and longer and louder and funkier and nastier and more misogynistically and more homophobically than Slim Shady ever thought he could. Shit, I could make P-Diddy sound like Pooh-Doody.

The real me can talk to the Queen about her latest hat while toeing someone's crotch under the elaborately set table for two hundred, and I'd be so smooth no one would be wiser—except for the object of my toe. The real me can chat with Tony Blair about the Queen's hat and still hold the attention of Ariel Sharon who's waiting for my advice on the Middle East.

The real me has a basketball tucked under one arm, holding a baseball in one hand, a golf club in the other, a soccerball at one foot and a surfboard under the other. And I can work those instruments of pride and power like soft pasta over a plastic fork. I'm a God of Sports. I'm a God of Scoring. I'm the Object of Bets Made. I will be on a Card that's traded years from now for a hundred thousand dollars.

The real me doesn't try to be like my brother, father, preacher, mailman, a.v. teacher, shop instructor, or my high school principal (who had a lisp and was having an affair with the Mexican American cafeteria worker/cook who refused to make enchiladas for the school because she didn't have her Green Card and that might give her away).

So I don't know who this freak is that looks back at me in the mirror, but it's not me. I'm someone so different than that. Go ahead, ask my ego. He'll tell you . . .

Monologue for a Rhino

ERROL BRAY

MAN enters holding aloft something small between finger and thumb. He holds it through most of the monologue. He has a TV Guide *in his back pocket. He speaks directly to the audience.*

MAN: I found a diamond today. Here under the rug. My . . . boarder? . . . House-mate? He left today and it seemed a good time to sweep things and keep busy with . . . the house. People don't stay with me very long. I should be a better man and I have tried to improve, but I'm not exactly artistic or sensitive or intellectual.

In this day and age men are supposed to weep at the drop of a hat . . . but I don't. I am a man and men do not cry. I've been to see a counselor and he didn't think I was a bad man because I didn't cry. She—my woman—made me go to the counselor. She who owned the diamond. Another failed attempt to improve me.

My life is . . . not exciting. I work in a big department store. Selling crockery. Not exciting. I do have one really good friend—a best friend you could say. Television! It never goes out and leaves me on my own. It doesn't get cranky if you turn it off or even if you go to sleep watching it. It's always there whenever you press that button. And it tells you things. There's documentaries and news. Even the ads tell you about sales and new products. You see all those countries around the world that you'd never be able to visit. (*Getting really enthusiastic.*) It makes you laugh. Sometimes it almost brings me to tears. You see kids starving. That can bring me close to tears. I don't know why people attack TV all the time. It's the best cure for loneliness anyone ever invented. It's the most important communications medium in existence. It documents the human condition, our triumphs and our disasters. Television is the global town crier. Television is my best friend . . . There—I've admitted it.

The damn diamond. I have to tell about that, don't I? Her and me—we'd been fighting for six months, non-stop. Usually it boiled down to the fact that I was inadequate in some way—mentally, morally, physically . . . yes, sexually. My job was hopeless, house was terrible, clothes dreadful, conversation boring . . . You get the picture? I wasn't good enough for her. She stood over here and yelled at me for half an hour. She yelled all the things she'd been telling me since the day we got engaged. She only accepted my proposal because she thought she could change me. (*Acts the speech out—shouting; almost screaming.*) "You are the most pathetic excuse for a man I have ever met. You think strong and silent still means masculine, don't you? You're only silent because you're too stupid to have any opinions or ideas. You're hardly intelligent enough to watch television. The advertisements are too subtle for you. Your body—disgusts me. I would rather masturbate than have sex with you."

(*Pause. He is almost out of breath. He keeps acting out the moves while holding the diamond between his fingers.*)

Then, she took off the ring and threw it on the floor. She turned dramatically . . . and made a dramatic exit. Three hours later, when I came out of the coma that her hatred had caused in me, I picked up the ring and tossed it in the garbage bin. I didn't look at it; didn't notice that the diamond had been knocked out of it. Knocked out, like I was knocked out. (*Slumps; defeated.*) And now I've found it and remembered her hatred . . . and mine. I hated myself. I believed everything she said. It wasn't an argument, it was a documentary . . . like television. She knew me. No one else had ever known me so well. She had to be right. I am not a worthy person. The air I breathe is wasted . . . So that's the diamond. (*Takes out a handkerchief and carefully wraps up the diamond and puts it in his pocket.*)

But I never cried. Whatever she said. Not a drop. I don't cry. It's not a manly thing. Crying. (*Takes a deep breath, then becomes cheery.*) Where's my friend? (*Takes* TV Guide *from back pocket.*) Time to sit with my friend. Where's my best friend? (*Leaves as he looks through the* TV Guide.)

is this it?

MATTIAS BRUNN

A man, mid-twenties, addresses the audience.

MAN: So. Is this it? If it is, then I don't know what to do with myself. Or anyone else for that matter.

I've got this anger inside. I'm trying to ignore it, but it keeps coming back to me. In a few seconds I'm going to have to kill somebody. Or myself. The anger has to go away.

The situation is this. I'm 26, I've got my college diploma, I've got the job I always wanted, and I earn more money than both my parents together. I'm gay but I haven't got the JT Leroy experience of filth. I've been through the coming-out process and I live my life with a man who says he loves me. We've got an apartment downtown, and everybody in the house or in our circle of friends look upon us as the golden couple—the successful gay couple.

I've reached the top, the peak, the highest high.

So now what?

Lately, I started to hate my situation. I'm not sure anymore. I don't know. I really don't. What now? What happens next? What the fuck am I going to do with myself and the rest of my life? If you have a dream, and fulfilled it—what do you do?

I have been thinking about this for about six months now, and I've come to at least two conclusions. Maybe three. One: I don't love my husband anymore. Two: I don't like any of my friends. And yes. Maybe three: I don't think I like my life anymore. Without goal—nothing. Goals are the meaning of life. Without them, the anger eats you up. Slowly, bit by bit.

I told my therapist all this, and I also told him how other people react to this. Mom for instance, said: "It's not possible for a man in your position to feel like this. You've got it all, haven't you?" But I do feel like this. I do. I really, really do. My life is worth nothing. The reply from my therapist was this: "Get yourself a hobby. A hobby creates goals. Or work out." Well. I already work out. So now what. A hobby? If you're thinking about killing yourself, what's a hobby worth to you? Nothing. Not a single thing.

So. This is what I'm thinking. I have to do something radical to create a new direction for my life. One—Divorce. Two—Quit the job. Three—risk my life. (*Pause. He picks up a coin out of his pocket.*) See this coin? This coin will help me come to a final decision. This coin will tell me if I'm going to kill myself and end this misery before it has gone too far. I've lived my life the way I wanted. Why go on? Of course, that's only one side of the coin. The other side gives me a hobby. Kind of bizarre, of course, but out of higher risk comes more satisfaction. The bizarre side, head, tells me not to kill myself, but somebody else. Or two. Maybe more. That creates the hobby and the hobby makes the anger and the dislikes go away.

To plan, to kill, and to get away with it. Therapy.

So. My own life or someone else's. Head or coin. Massacre or mute. Ready? Here we go . . . One, two, three! (*He flips the coin. Blackout.*)

The Actor

CHONG TZE CHIEN

ACTOR: I thought I should begin my audition piece . . . by telling a joke. Yes, yes I know. "Just get on with your piece" you might be thinking. But bear with me. People love jokes. It's the perfect icebreaker. Ease the tension. Relax the muscles. Create a value-free environment. Not that I don't want you to make the selection and exercise some creative judgment. You are gods.

OK, I may seem a little high-strung. But that's because I want the role so much, SO MUCH! I am peeing in my pants just thinking about it! I'm perfect for the part! You just have to see it! If you would allow me to show you my moves! I have excellent moves! . . . Of course, I shouldn't use the word *move*. It's not a very apt word to use in an audition, is it? Unless I am talking about my skills in bed . . . But I digress.

I'm sorry. SO SORRY. I AM a little distracted. I just broke up with my girlfriend, you see. Just at the door. OK, I'm lying. Three years ago. Now, she has seen my *moves, if you know what I mean*. . . . No, no, I know what you are thinking. I DIDN'T stink in bed. That wasn't why she left. MY MOVES were excellent.

Yes . . . on with the joke. It's very funny. I can assure you of that. Because it would be disastrous if it isn't. OH MY GOD, I would really stink if that happens, WOULDN'T I?? You would just politely look away and pretend to scribble something on my audition form and pray, AND PRAY that my time is up soon so that you can tell me, "THANK YOU FOR AUDITIONING, YOU WERE EXCELLENT!!!" when the subtext, the SUBTEXT is "DON'T CALL US, WE'LL CALL YOU!"

I KNOW SUBTEXT! I KNOW REJECTION! I AM AN ACTOR, YOU DON'T HAVE TO PATRONIZE ME!! I AM NOT GAY!!!

Perhaps I gave away too much information over there. Not that I think being gay is . . . to be ashamed of. I mean . . . I have many gay friends. I work in a profession known for attracting these people . . .When I say "these people," I don't mean it in a disparaging way. Of course not. I mean, why blow my chances when I'm sure many of you behind the desk are gay . . . or not. Not that it matters. IT'S COOL. MY BROTHER IS GAY!!! AND I LOVE HIM!

Of course he doesn't have a choice in that. We're family after all, despite *everything*. Besides, it doesn't run in the family. My mum and pa aren't. I know I am not. Because people say that we always grow up to be our parents. Because I believe that. Because I will get married and have children like every bloke. And because I hate them. I hate the clothes they wear, the way they talk, the new-age, sensitive men they portray. They are every girl's best friend. They might as well become their dogs for all I care.

It's true, isn't it? The most successful, richest and beautiful men in the world today are fags. They are creative, funny, smart. My ASS! They have taken my looks, my pussies, my pride, my dick. Where do I stand? I might as well let them take my ass and fuck me all over, the man, the real one in the family.

My brother is the big-shot lawyer of the family. While I never get a second call back at auditions. But all the best actors in this world are fags. And I am a good actor. I am the best actor in this world. I fool everyone. Until . . . my girlfriend, the love of my life, caught me in bed with another guy. I was so mad, I screamed at her, hit her on the face and threw her out. Who enters without knocking first? There is no basic courtesy anymore. No more, not on that day, not from that day onwards. Courtesy is dead. Because on that very same day, I went to my brother's 30th surprise birthday party. When he came through the door in the dark, I threw a punch at him. I broke his nose and arm. He cried like a bloody fag, a bloody fag. Pathetic. And it's my girlfriend's fault. She screwed me up. I used to be polite.

It's hell being a heterosexual nowadays.

So ladies and gentleman, the million dollar joke is this: I actually forgot to prepare an audition piece. So I thought I should tell you my life story, thus far, instead. Now, you must admit, it's a funny joke.

Gone

JOEL MURRAY

NILS: I'm going 'cuz I'm going and I have to get gone now I'm—you don't get it—I'm suffocating and I don't take passengers I don't even love you yet enough to make you cry I just woke up like I was in a closed casket so that's that I didn't want this to happen to me this time but it happened and it happened so please stop your goddamned crying.
(*Turns and starts to exit. Stops. Returns. Tenderly.*)
    Darla. Ssshhh-ssshhh. All right, all right. Christ on toast. It's not you. I move. Okay? I'm . . . I just have to keep like . . . dodging. It's not you. Being cried over, man, that's . . . Thank you. Sweetie, you got a big snot running down your nose. Other side. That's it. See . . . It's—goddamnit. My parents. I saw the end of my parents coming long before it happened.
    So I moved out and just kept moving. I move even if it's right next door to where I'm living. At this one apartment building, I moved in downstairs. Then three months later, I moved upstairs. And before you could say "strange," I moved downstairs again. Not even in the same downstairs place. I can't do that.
    My mother and father used to move all the time. Spent most of their lives packing and unpacking. Actually, it was a weird sorta sign that everything was okay between them. "Always a new beginning," they used to say. But then it started to get desperate. You know? Ugly. Because each time they moved, they had more stuff to take with them. And that was the beginning of the end.
    They started accumulating more and more stuff, so they

couldn't move as fast. They'd spend all their time packing and unpacking, because they couldn't let go of any of their stuff. They started out with a half-empty Ford Fairlane station wagon and ended up with two jam-packed eighteen-wheeler Mayflower moving trucks.

What it was, I guess, is that when they had nothing, they seemed to be in love. Anyway the more stuff they got, the more they seemed not to be in love. Man. They had stuff everywhere. The inside of their house looked like an obsessive-compulsive's jamboree. Dad got overwhelmed by it all and started hiding in all the stuff and mom could never find him.

Once I found him under the roll top of his island-sized rolltop desk. He was curled up humming "Chances Are," making lists of things that he thought were going wrong in his life. He told me he felt pretty sure he could make a comeback if he and mom could keep moving. I said to him, I said, "Dad, this is your chance. You and Mom. You two might really have something if you stayed put and tried to figure it out." But his mind was somewhere else on purpose. He knew he had gotten married to someone that made it like, you know, living in a slaughterhouse. But he'd rather stay with her than be without her. But it was just . . . she could have been anybody. He needed somebody. It didn't matter who.

And Mom knew it, too. She knew it cold. He was a, you know, a butcher for her just like she was for him. So she just wanted to keep moving. That way they could both pretend that the future held something it didn't; that all of a sudden they would find themselves with the person they loved for being that person and not for being just a, a symbol, or a—no, not a symbol . . . a substitute, you know, like a, a permanent stand-in for someone they could really be in love with.

Well, anyway, Dad never did make his comeback, so they had to stop moving. Instead, Mom started having additions put on the house. One room had a set of stairs that led to nothing but the ceiling, because they went broke. Last time I saw her, she was sitting on those stairs that don't lead anywhere hoping to at least settle for Dad to make a comeback.

Ahhh. They couldn't keep running from themselves anyway.

You know, I used to think . . . if I got lost, then I'd really find something. But . . . I've always been lost.

You don't have to say anything, Darla. I didn't mean to . . . you know. Just look at it this way: The farther away I get, the closer I'll be. Huh? (*Smiles.*)

But for now, I'm better off gone.

Drug Rep

MATTHEW NADER

A Drug Company Representative for Roboxacin is talking to another rep at a Chili's/Applebee's-type restaurant. He is irritatingly nice. Someone you'd politely talk to because of his or her niceness, but you wish they would leave you alone.

DRUG REP: (*Yawns.*) Don't make me yawn . . . Y'know, I get so tired some of these days, sometimes I just wanna be able to take a quick nap. Recharge the batteries. (*Laughs.*)

You don't know how many times I've just gotten into my car, I pop the seat back, and zone out for a bit. I set my cell phone to wake me up, and after a couple of minutes, I'm good as new. Listen. I get tired if I work all day. It's just a simple fact. You know, there are many times when I'm driving home on the highway, the visor in my car's only blocking half the sun, and I start to do "the nod." And that's dangerous! I've pulled over to the side of the turnpike many, many times. I sleep for a bit, then I get back on and drive for a bit. (*It's no big deal.*)

Ehhh. I can fall asleep just about anywhere. I could fall asleep right here if you gave me enough time. In fact, I think I have fallen asleep here before. (*Beat.*) Let me tell you an embarrassing story.

One afternoon, I was tired. So I pulled over and parked in the parking lot of some bank. I went to sleep. And when I woke up, I saw the bank's building right in front of me. Since I was in my car, I thought I had dozed off while driving and was about to hit the bank. I grabbed my steering wheel with all my might and tried to veer it away from the building. That's when I realized I was in "park." I kinda looked around and made sure no one had seen me freak out. I'll tell ya, my heart was beating so fast all the way home and for the rest of the night.

So, yeah, have you by chance . . . heard anything about, uh, me getting the ol' (*Wraps an imaginary noose around his neck and hangs himself, tongue spilling out.*). Because a little bluebird whispered in my ear some top-secret information that heads are gonna start . . . doing that spinning thing . . . (*Correcting.*) Right! Rolling. (*Pointing to his head.*) And you know, this head is pretty round! So, I just wanna know what you know. Because I have no clue what I've done wrong.

Nothing. I'm up four percent this week. You know what a giant leap that is? I've made some valuable relationships with many of the doctors in this whole tri-state area, all in the name of Roboxacin! And their staffs, most of them look forward to seeing me. I bring them their little gifts, Neosect pens, Medi-Highlighters, oatmeal cookies, and chocolate! They can't help but like me, right? I'm giving them things. That should buy their respect. I mean, I don't know about you, but I've often been accused of being too nice. (*Scoffs.*) Like that's a problem. (*Beat.*) That can't be it. Right?

You like me, don't you? I showed you the ropes. But I'm not like, irritatingly nice, right? I'm courteous, yet pleasant. And I can be really funny, ask the Endo-nurse in Lost Valley. I put the charm face on every day. (*Reaches in pocket.*) You wanna try a Prilotect? It's the only thing that's gonna help me through this day. (*Takes pill. It pleases him momentarily.*) I'm a likable character, right?

Double

BRIAN NELSON

BRIAN: Okay, I don't know how long your answering machine runs, but I'll just take a chance here. This is Brian Nelson calling. THE REAL ONE. No, I know, you're real, too. I assume. Look, we have the same name, and I've been thinking about it a long time now. I've avoided watching you for years. Which sometimes was not easy. But one day I'm in an apartment in Berlin, the only English station is CNN, so I have it on for company while I'm working, and suddenly I hear the announcer saying, "In Atlanta, here's Brian Nelson." Now, I know I'm in Berlin. Not Atlanta. And then you come on the screen and start reading the headlines. I don't listen to any of it because I'm just shocked, the little title at the bottom of the screen says "Brian Nelson."

I thought: This is like a Poe story, here's my doppelganger, except he's older than I am, his face has more lines, I would never wear a suit like that and I'm cuter overall, THANK GOD FOR THAT. But I keep watching, and my name stays on the screen, it's hard to argue with CNN, and CNN is saying YOU'RE Brian Nelson. I wanted to check my driver's license and make sure I'm still me. But I have more faith in myself than that. Really I do. Yet it bugs me. This stealing my name.

It's especially annoying because my middle name is Keith, and so I had to grow up listening to stupid jokes about Brian Keith. "How's it going, Uncle Bill?" Yuk yuk yuk. I asked my mother why she had to give me a famous person's name. She lamely explained he wasn't famous when I was born. PLAN

AHEAD, I wanted to say. But Brian Keith fortunately died, and so I was spared all that. Until you came along.

Not that it's all your fault. I'm well aware, perhaps you aren't, that there are still other Brian Nelsons out there. When we bought our house, I had to explain to the loan officers that I wasn't the Brian Nelson who owed child support. (That isn't you, is it?) And when I rent a video, I have to distinguish myself from SEVERAL people named Brian Nelson. You wouldn't think it would be that common a name, would you? Yet these men live within driving distance of me, apparently, frequent the same video store—maybe the stranger thing is, why do I never run into them? Who are all these men, living lives with my name? Do they know about me? Are they bothered that I have their name? NO, I TAKE ISSUE WITH THAT, IT'S *MY* NAME. I AM UNIQUE. AND I AM NOT THREATENED BY ANY OF THIS.

Now, I want to point out, I called your secretary earlier today, and she advised me that someone named Brian Nelson has been harassing you. Stalking you. I mention this to make it clear that I am NOT that Brian Nelson. I would never stalk anyone. Some people seem to think I walk around mad all the time, but I'm just thinking a lot, right? I'm not the restraining order type. But the thing is, one day I typed my name into a Google search string, and I couldn't believe how many Brian Nelson links there were! And none of them were me. But most of 'em weren't you, either. Which made me wonder if we aren't in the same boat. Are you also haunted by those other guys out there with our name? Maybe we should get to know each other. I could get to Atlanta now and then. Wouldn't it be fun if we were friends? We could go out on double dates and drive everybody crazy, people'd say "Brian" and we'd both say "What?" Well, we don't have to do that. Unless you think it would be fun. Either way. Look, I've left my number with your secretary about seventeen times, give me a call. It could be a hoot. Come on! Come on! WHAT THE HELL!

Remember: NOT the stalking Brian Nelson. NOT the one who owes child support, either. And not you! Ha! Okay um okay okay. GOODBYE, "BRIAN!" JUST CALL, OKAY?

A Joke on the New Guy

DAN NIELSEN

ANDOR, 18, is wearing a beat-up army coat with a large "Impeach Nixon" button, and a bandanna with a "peace" sign. His hair and the shoulders of his coat are wet.

SCENE: A street with houses.

TIME: A Monday morning in the autumn of 1969.

ANDOR: Sally! Christ! Open the door! (*Sees her through the screen.*) Hi babe. Look, I know I'm supposed to be at work, but I quit—walked off. Yeah, "just like that." "Just like that" is how important things get done. And I figure I've got about three minutes before your dad comes looking for me. And before you ask, that's gasoline you smell. I'm soaked in it. That's why I'm here . . . You look great by the way. I think I like you better pregnant . . . at least so far. (*A long, awkward silence, then:*) Sally, I didn't sign the letter. I tore it up. I know the lawyer said in the letter that if I marry you I don't have to go to Vietnam—but it just seems so wrong. I mean . . . it's not my kid, is it? Do the math. We were broke up when it happened. I can't just lie about something like that. (*Takes a pint bottle from his pocket and has a swallow.*)

You want a sip? . . . Wait, no! That can't be good for the baby. And you have to stop smoking, too. Anyway, a lighted match wouldn't be such a good idea. With the gasoline and all I could go up like one of those protest monks—which brings me to how I got here. (*Stands, takes another drink, and relives the experience as he narrates.*)

Today was my first day on the job, right? All I had to do was keep the forklifts filled with gas. So, a driver gave me the signal—I ran over with the five-gallon can, put the funnel in, and started to pour. In an instant, it fucking overflowed. It was a setup—the tank was full. Found out it's a joke they play on the new guy. Sally, they were laughing at me. I was yanking on the funnel. It came loose and landed on my head. . . . I'm sure I looked like the Tin Man in the *Wizard of Oz* . . . I couldn't see. I couldn't breathe. I couldn't help it . . . I started crying. God, I cry so easy . . . a lot of help I'd be in a war. Anyway, Kenny, the foreman, pointed me toward the wash-up room. I made a wrong turn and walked right past your dad's office. He saw me. He saw everything. (*Another awkward moment.*)

I ran. I ran all the way here. And I'm not stopping either. I'm leaving. I'm going to Canada. Sally, you know me, I've wanted to be a draft dodger since I was like a sophomore. This is my one chance. And it's not that I don't want to marry you. I do, I do want to marry you. I just don't have to marry you, which makes me want to marry you even more. And . . . I want you to leave with me right now. We'll start a whole new life together. We can do whatever we want. We can be whoever we want. I want to be your husband . . . and the father of your . . . of our child, but not here . . . not like this. Christ! That's your dad's car! I love you, Sally! Whattya say? Gasoline and all, will you come with me?

Booker-T Is Back in Town

DAN STROEH

PALMER stands center stage. He could be wearing mechanic's coveralls. He's in his late twenties, athletic, handsome. He speaks with a hint of a Midwestern twang. In Palmer's little town, he is the man of the hour, and he has told this story many times (by request), so he's getting pretty good at it:

PALMER: Booker-T is back in town. Did you hear? I was the first one to talk to him. First one to see him; walking into the Tastee Diner, just like I remember him: Torn-up, faded army jacket. Big old backpack slung over those bony shoulders. Bushy beard, looking like a—I don't know—big ol' gray rat that attached itself to his face and died. I was in the Tastee Diner having lunch—a late lunch 'cause I left early yesterday and had to finish replacing the brakepads on some damn teenager's fucking beat-up junker before he got outta school— and I'm sitting there eating lunch at like two, when Booker-T walks in the door. And at first, nobody sees him. Nobody except me, of course. And I'm like, shit. It's Booker-T. And he walks over next to that big sign on the counter that says, "Have some chili with your meal" and he says, "You folks sell chili?"

And I laugh a little. 'Cause, you know, he's standing right next to the sign, and he looks over at me and he says, "Well, I'll be damned. Palmer Madison. In the flesh. You still live here? I used to watch you play ball, boy. Best quarterback I ever seen. How you been? You still play ball?"

And I look at him the way I look at people when they ask me if I still play ball. Like I'm pissed off that they brought it up, even though I'm not. I squint up my eyes, and I clench my teeth and I stare, before they start throwing around words like "all-state" and "MVP" and "rushing record." It's a look that says, "No, asshole. I don't play ball any more." He musta thought that look meant I didn't know who he was, though, 'cause he says, "You don't know who I am? I'm Booker-T. You ask your folks about me. You ask anyone. You tell 'em Booker-T's back in town."

And I say, "I know who you are, Booker-T."

Booker-T says he come home to settle down. And he tells me a story about being in New York City, right after nine-one-one, you know? Apparently they got a statue of that dude from *The Honeymooners* outside the bus station, okay, and Booker-T's sitting there at his feet smoking a Swisher Sweet. (I guess he can loiter in a big city as easy as he can in a little town.) So he's just sitting there, smoking and talking to him-self—you know, like he always does—and some dude from North Carolina runs up and asks him for money. This dude tells Booker-T that he's got a mother in the hospital down in Raleigh, and all his shit was in the towers, and he can't reach nobody to wire him money and he needs to get down to see his mom 'cause she's on her deathbed and all, so he's trying to find fifty bucks for bus fare. Well, Booker-T don't have too many soft spots, but one of them, I guess, is sick mothers. And another one is dutiful sons. So Booker-T reaches into his wallet and pulls out forty-seven dollars and twenty-three cents. Everything he has. And the dude from North Carolina stands there with Booker-T's money in his hand. He hesitates, and then he says thank you, and runs off and buys a bus tick-et. Comes back, gives Booker-T a buck seventeen in change then takes Booker-T's P.O. Box number so he can mail him a check once he gets his affairs in order. Then the dude from North Carolina heads off and catches his bus home to his sick Mama in Raleigh. Well, apparently, Booker-T, other than being out forty-six-oh-six, forgets about it. Last week, though, Booker-T finds a letter in his mailbox. It says, "Dear Sir, thank you for your kindness. Got home just before Mom passed." No signature. No return address. And enclosed there's a check for ten thousand dollars. So Booker-T takes that check, hides it in his copy of the *King James Bible*, and he hitchhikes home. Here.

Booker-T asks me why I never left town. Never went to college or nothing. I tell him I was thinking of joining up with the Marines after nine-one-one, but I never got around to it. Booker-T says we're both local legends and that makes us similar cats, me and him. Cut from the same cloth. But I say that's bullshit. And I'm like, damn, if I had ten thousand dollars, I wouldn't come back here. (*He sighs.*)

Course, I guess I'd never give some guy all my cash just 'cause he say he got a sick mother in Raleigh, neither.

Fam-ug-ily

All this "bro" talk. Who the hell's my bro? Guy on the street last night bumps into me, nearly slices me in half with his sharp elbow, keeps walking but tosses back over his head, "Sorry about that, bro." Do I want to tackle him on the street and grind his face into the cement because he's delivered a death blow to my torso, or is it the assumed intimacy in that short burst of "bro" that makes me crazy?

In that instant, he's made me family. I'm his "bro," brother because . . . well, because we both have a dick and walk upright with a handy set of opposing thumbs. It's no big deal, I guess; it's just a word tossed off. But if we really were in the same family, I'd be comfortable enough to say, "You stupid asshole. You nearly punctured my spleen with your elbow. And just because you played football and I didn't, and just because dad always liked you more and called you 'son' and called me 'hey,' and just because mom always says you were the easy birth and I was the real labor, and just because you've always dated not one, not two but three girls at the same time and I can't get the biggest loser/nerd/virgin-forever in the school to even smile at me, and just because you have straight, blonde hair and blue eyes and white teeth and a dimple—a fuckin' unjust dimple—square in the middle of your chin and I look like the love child of Madeline Albright and Gene Wilder, and just because you broke both legs and an arm and a wrist when you went waterskiing and got all that attention and I fell down a flight a stairs and people just jumped over me and got pissed off because I was in the way, does not give you the right to think you're better than me . . . I'm the only one that can do that, and I do it pretty damn often."

Ohhhhhhhhhhhh, this family thing. It can be fam-ug-ily.

83

Competence

BARTON BISHOP

A hotel balcony in St. Simons Island, Georgia.

PHIL: Okay, okay! Mom! Jesus! You gonna listen to me, or—? *Listen.* I am not . . . asking you . . . for money. For . . . Okay, I *am* asking you for money, but—Please take that disapproving look off your face, Mom, please, you have had it there since I was fifteen, and I can't—This is not—I don't need rent money. I'm fine, it's not like I need . . . Seriously, and this is not one of my—What do you like calling them? Get-rich-quick schemes? Well, it's none of those, I'm through with that kind of thing. Honestly. I'm going about things, you know, the whole "normal" way, and I'm doing fine. I swear. But I do need some money. For . . . It . . . It's for the doctor. I need to see a doctor. Don't worry. Not sick. I mean . . . Not really. I don't know, I might be, I . . . That's what I have to—Ah, man, I'm going about this all wrong, I, um . . . Okay. Okay. I met a girl, mom. (*Pause.*) She's . . . amazing. Beautiful. Smart. Funny. And the best thing? She doesn't think I'm a loser, she . . . You know. Thinks I got it going on. For some reason. (*Pause.*) Maybe this is the part where you say, um, "Congratulations, Phil," or "Tell me more, Phil." (*Pause.*) "I'm happy for you, Phil." (*Pause.*) No? Okay. Well. Know that it's good. Except that . . . You see . . . Certain, um . . . *things* . . . are not working. Properly. As they . . . You know . . . Should. And I don't know why. I don't know if it's because I've been depressed for so long or—I mean, I don't even know if I *am* depressed, I mean by the clinical definition, with chemicals and neurons and stuff actually breaking down or apart or whatever they do, or if there's actually something, um, *physical*, you know, just a leak in the pipes or something. I don't know how these things work. But that's what I have to find out, because Kelly—That's the girl. I mean, she's really patient and understanding about it all, you know, she's fine doing . . . other things. Jesus, I can't believe I'm talking to my mother about this. Wow. Okay. This is embarrassing for me too, you know. I'm twenty-seven, I should be like a lumberjack, right, I should . . . But I'm not. And I don't have health insurance, so it's not like I can just waltz into the doctor's office and say, "I have a problem, fix me." I can't even afford an initial visit. And I'm sure they're gonna wanna check everything out, you know, send me to a shrink, to a prostate guy, back over to the shrink, and I can't afford all that. And, you know, despite what women say, it *does* matter. Okay? It *does*. So before you go thinking anything, just know that I have already been in situations where, you know, at first, she's like, "Oh, no, it's fine, I understand," and then after a while, she's suddenly accusatory, she's all, "You're just not attracted to me," or "I think you're gay and you just don't know it," or whatever because, whether she wants to admit it or not, she wants sex, she wants to get nailed, she wants hard, lasting-for-hours porno fucking, and I can't give that to her so suddenly all the other shit, all the supposed feelings and admirations and good times, it's all disposable, you know, it doesn't mean anything because I can't get a fucking hard-on! (*Pause.*) I'm sorry. That isn't . . . You don't wanna hear that. I know. It's just . . . It's one of those things I keep all bottled up. So when I start talking about it . . . I mean . . . Mom . . . It's been going on for so long that . . . I don't know if I can't get an erection because I'm depressed or if I'm just depressed because I can't get an erection. I don't know anymore. But I want to. I don't wanna be embarrassed about it, I just wanna go to the doctor, find out what's wrong with me. Because I think . . . I *think*. I'm pretty close to being happy. For the first time in a really long time. And I don't want something stupid like this getting in the way anymore. Mom . . . Please . . . I called Dad, he won't even call me back. Okay? You're the only person I can go to . . . Will you help me?

86

a bone close to my brain

DAN DIETZ

A MAN stands beside an easel with a large white pad on it; he uncaps a marker and draws a big tooth on the paper.

MAN:
today my brother is a dentist
he knows all about these little bones
huddling tight inside your mouth
incisors, bicuspids, wisdoms way in the back
he knows them all
their shapes and contours
their uses and misuses
the damage they can reasonably take
from impact or decay
my brother is a dentist today

i don't mean he just got certified
i don't mean he opened a practice
i mean that today my brother is a dentist
just like yesterday he was a radiologist
and last month he was a reporter for the *new york times*
only two things about him stay the same
day in, day out
his address, this tidy little house in new jersey
which we've shared for the nine years
since our parents passed away
and the fact that i am his big brother
no matter what else he erases and remakes
inside his mind
these two facts sit solid and bonehard

within his head

he can't feed himself
he doesn't grasp the need to fuel his body
he can't bathe himself
left on his own, he'll either starve or stink himself to death
he doesn't live in his skin, his stomach, his fingernails
he lives here
in the bulbous gray organ
just above and behind
the roof of his mouth
that's his house

(MAN *draws a roof and windows on the tooth, maybe even a chimney with a curlicue of smoke.*)

the rest of him
skin, stomach, fingernails
is like a yard

(*He draws a yard by the house.*)

a yard that needs a full-time, round the clock landscaper
to keep from going to hell
that's me
i tend him
he trusts me
anyone else comes near the yard
(skin, stomach, fingernails)
he screams, hits, bites
gets arrested, gets bailed out, forgets, etc.
but not me
he would never hurt me

except for today
today he will hurt me

in about ten minutes
he will walk in here
lay me down on this chair
and tear out of my head
a single, white, completely healthy
tooth

(*He flips to a new sheet, draws a new tooth.*)

and i will let him

i can't get used to the way teeth look
strange
spiny
like they belong on the outside
of some prehistoric fish
not sprouting from my face
maybe i should smile more
but i was always that way
even as a kid
i can't find one picture of me
smiling showing my teeth
always just a twist of the lips
to indicate a grin

gerald always smiled with teeth
he's smiling right now
in the kitchen, sterilizing his instruments
which consist of a penlight
and a pair of pliers

he's brilliant
he learns this stuff in just hours
pores over textbooks
random ones i pick up
from the public library

to keep his house

(*He draws a roof on the tooth, draws a yard.*)

occupied

(*Draws a happy stick figure waving from the house.*)

he dives into the volumes
(the only medication he'll accept)
and the next time i see him
he's completely reborn
he's memorized it all
he's a dentist
(radiologist, reporter)
and he can't remember a day
when he wasn't a dentist
(radiologist, reporter)

he was reading tolstoy at age eight
studying fractals at eleven
those huge numbers
blooming out infinite all over the place
numbers that want to be pictures
he called them

what does a number do
if it wants to be a picture

he grew into adolescence
his head devouring everything
like his eyes were mouths
awards, acclaim
the "g" word tossed about
(and i don't mean "gerald")
by people important enough to believe

he was slated to graduate high school
before his sixteenth birthday

then mom and dad died
when our house
got broken into

(*Draws a hole on the house and an arrow pointing into the hole.*)

attempted robbery
became
attempted rape
became

i was away at college
i didn't have to come downstairs
didn't have to try to stop it
try to save
but gerald

he was fifteen
the same age as the boy
they caught and convicted
after finding his skin cells
beneath my mother's

i moved back home
took a break from school
gerald however refused to take a break
so close to graduation
less than a year
but the things he started saying
and doing

it was like his mind had twisted
to indicate a person

(Points to the person waving from the house.)

a person
that wants to be a picture
and he'll erase and try again
until he gets the picture
right

he's beautiful at night
he sits in his room
soft light
pages blurring by

he was expelled
for tearing open a substitute's blouse
he insisted she was in danger
her beat was irregular
he could hear it across the room
he had to press his stethoscope
to her bare chest
to be sure

silly
tragic moments are always
so fucking silly

like this one
today

(Flips to a new sheet, draws a new tooth.)

today my little brother
will remove my tooth
which he is convinced
upon examination with his penlight
is rife with decay

(Draws holes on the tooth.)

little holes
in a bone close to my brain

he will administer anesthetic
a rag steeped in ether
(which he got from god knows where)
and pluck out my tooth
("pluck" is probably not
the right word)
and smile
believing
he has saved me from danger
i will give him this belief
today

and tomorrow
i will take him to a place
where they will administer
a more sophisticated anesthetic
one which will
maybe
combined with other treatments
over the course of years
help

tomorrow
i will turn him over to people
who will break into his house

*(Draws a roof on the tooth, draws a yard, draws arrows pointing
into the holes in the tooth.)*

and do their best
as he flails and screams

to clean the damn thing up

i will leave him there
i will erase him and

because i can't i

you wake up one day
and the decay

i can't find myself
in this picture

i will leave him there
and return here

(*Turns to a fresh blank page.*)

to my house

and gerald
i know
will hold onto my tooth
forever
a bone close to my brain
perhaps it will reside
beneath his pillow
as he sleeps
giving him dreams
of his big brother
crying "don't hate me"

don't hate me

and perhaps
somewhere in the back of my mouth

i will feel the head
of my little brother shift
in the night
every night
after
tonight.

Take a Load Off

GARY GARRISON

LLOYD is talking to his older brother, Danny, on a loading dock.

LLOYD: Sit down. Take a load off, Danny. This won't take long. Give me five minutes and you're off with your crew, throwing back a beer, I promise . . . So, yeah, I don't know what's got into me, Danny, but I feel like I'm really taking care of business. You know that old guy on the bus that I told you about that's got a tumor on his nose and is always making with the nose jokes? I look at him today, right in the eye, and I say, "Your jokes are fuckin' gross because your nose is gross. So stop with the jokes, okay? Everyone's try to eat their fuckin' Egg McMuffin and you're on and on about your nose." The guy was, like, silent. Like a tomb. Like I shot 'em or some-thing. Then the whole bus applauds me—even the driver. (*Topping that.*)

And then last night, I finally took care of those drag queens that live above me. They've been wettin' their pants to give me a perm for a year. So I go up, I bang on their door to tell them to turn down the fuckin' Mariah Carey *Glitter* sound track 'cause I've heard that shit till I'm ready to puke, and they start in on me with the perm. And I say, "Look, girls, you're sweet as you can be, but I don't want a fuckin' perm. I hardly have any hair left, and no, I don't want to borrow one of your fuckin' drag wigs. I mean, that's very nice of you and all, and yes, I'm sure you could comb it to look like a 50's Johnny Mathis, but at this point in my life, if I go bald it's the least of my problems." They're like, shocked. They're like, "okay, cool." Can you imagine? Me, who never says nothing to nobody about nothing, because . . . because I don't know why, but I don't. And all of a sudden, I'm fuckin' Rambo of the mouth. I'm, like, killing everybody off, one by one . . . Which brings me to you, big brother. (*A beat, then.*)

The people here at work, Danny, they don't respect me because you're my brother and you gave me this job and there were three people in line for it. And I don't care what you say, they haven't gotten "use" to me. And you know why? I don't know what I'm doing. And they all know that. Then I fuck up, you pick up after me, and they walk away thinking the same thing: he's just a fuck-up. Good thing his brother's around. It's been like that all our lives. And I got to wonder, why do you even bother? (*Harder.*) Like yesterday. Yesterday I ordered three hundred alloy steel, hollow head, set screw, wrench-sets. (*Presenting them.*)

And here they are! The manufacturer rush-ordered the alloy steel, hollow head, set screw, wrench-sets to me, 'cause I guess I said get it to me pronto 'cause our machinery's breaking down without the fuckin' alloy steel . . . things . . . And here's the problem, Danny. We don't have any machinery that uses these. But here's even a bigger problem: I don't remember even making the order, that's how messed up I am. And Don Olson, in Purchasing, comes to me fifteen minutes ago and says three hundred boxes of these things are at the loading gate and there's no one there to unload them, but that's okay because we don't use them anyway. And should he clean up after my ass one more time and send them back? Should he notify you of the return expense, or just cover it like he did last time? And I stupidly say to him, "Are you sure I ordered it? I don't even remember ordering it." And he says, "You're the only one that can authorize that." But I don't remember ordering this shit. (*Closer in.*)

And I'm walking down to the loading dock to re-load all of this crap onto the flatbed truck, and I'm thinking about it, see, and I think: Wait . . . You . . . You can order this shit! You can order these fuckin' alloy things, too! There's not one, there are two people who can authorize an order like that. And so I want to know, Danny. Your little brother's here, in your face, wantin' to know: Did you set me up, man? Did you? And if you did, why? (*Inches from his face.*)

And I got a theory, here. Was I starting to get too good? Was I working too hard, and too thorough, and on time, and on budget, and not making mistakes and making my mark? Was I finally making a better name for myself? And did that just scare the fuck out of you? You used to remind me, almost daily, "Nobody needs a loser around." But I think, Danny boy, I think that's exactly what you needed. (*Seeing someone else.*)

Hey, Carson! Can I have a word with you, my man? Next time I hear you say that shit about me growing breasts and needing a man-bra soon, I'm gonna punch your teeth out. Understand? (*Quietly.*) Ohhhh, I'm on a roll, Danny!

Drinking with Dad

ROBERT HENRY

STEVE, mid-30s or older, enters, holding a bottle of wine. He stops and looks at the audience.

STEVE: I just found this bottle in my wine cellar. A 1963 Chateau Palmer. It's a famous winery, maybe a little under-rated, usually—so it's only profoundly over-priced instead of being perversely over-priced. I inherited this bottle from my Dad—forgot he had two. We drank the other one together. (*More upbeat, enjoying this part of the memory.*)

See, he was the first guy on the block to drink wine. The story goes that when he came back from World War II after being stationed with a family in Luxembourg, he said to Mom, (*Bombastic tones.*) "Red"—(*His own voice.*) that was his nickname for her, Red. But by the time I was born her hair was gray, and it never made any sense to me. Anyways, he says, (*Bombastic.*) "Red, we've been eating and drinking like fools. You need to learn to cook, and I need to buy wine."

So Mom subscribed to *Gourmet*, Dad got her all the veal and cream she needed, and they never looked back. About every other month a big UPS truck would deliver cases of wine. Sometimes he'd buy special bottles for his cellar—he dug the damn thing out of the basement! He had the weirdest damn bunch of wines in it—and he never drank 'em. Well, finally towards the end he did. He'd cook sweetbreads or something and call me up: "Steven! Made my sweetbreads and drank that Burgundy you gave me! Delicious!"

When I got older I always got him wine for holiday presents, which he'd stick in the cellar. Then finally I stopped giving him wines to age and gave him ones he had to open right away. (*Enjoying the memory.*) Those damn bottles cost me a fortune! Try finding a 20-year-old Chave Hermitage! If he knew how much I spent on those bottles, he'd have freaked . . . Why didn't he ever drink those wines? . . . I found a 1929 white Burgundy he never drank. 1929. What was he waiting for? Dad, hello, drink the damn thing, will ya? (*Sadder, looking at the '63 Palmer.*)

He did drink this one, though . . . I brought Dad home from the hospital under hospice care. That means you don't go back to the hospital—you're as good as dead, and it's gonna hit you at home. A concept simultaneously civilized and morbid. So he gets home, under hospice care, riddled with cancers, and he decides that for dinner he wants a Tahitian Crab Sandwich from Trader Vic's. His favorite restaurant, went there twice a week because he owned a paint factory near the place. The waiters would stand over him, dip a napkin in water, and wipe paint pigment off the back of his neck. He loved to eat and drink, and they loved that he did both all the time at their restaurant. So I called the place, explained who it was for. They don't do take out, but for good ol' Al, well, no worries. Then I got down there and had to tell hostess Claudette that Dad wouldn't be in the restaurant again. She just hugged me and wept . . . I remember feeling her tears falling onto my neck. (*Holding back his own tears.*)

So I got the sandwiches—which are pretty vile, actually, a croissant with a lousy cheese sauce and thawed crabmeat. Dad asked if there was any Palmer left in the cellar. A year or two earlier he had opened a '79 Palmer I had given him, and he loved it—so why not have a Palmer now?! I found this baby. The '63. Doesn't go with crab? Who cares! '63 was a shitty year? So what! He ate a bite of the sandwich and drank a few slurps of the wine. (*Enjoying the irony.*) It was pretty bad wine. Weak nose, thin attack, no mid-palate, blahblahblah . . .

We didn't care at all. He sat there, in his hospital bed set up in the dining room because it had the best view, looking out at the garden and the pine trees . . . the nurse hovering nearby . . . She wanted to feed him the sandwich, but he was determined to feed himself. He lifted the glass: "Steven, by God it still tastes like grapes." He was right; it did. I sat with him until he fell asleep, and then the nurse and I lifted him into bed. It was the best bottle of wine I've ever had.

Family Man

PAUL LAMBRAKIS

I love kids. I want to have kids someday . . . at least one kid, anyway. It could happen, I mean, it already did. Once.

I used to have lots of girlfriends . . . Jesus, that seems like a lifetime ago when I think about it. Back then I used to think maybe this was a phase . . . I dunno, like something I needed to get outta my system. I thought the more women I fucked, the more I'd like it, kinda the same way you grow to like Scotch, or raw oysters. I mean, yeah, some guys say, "Sure, I been with women before, it was alright." But I used to chase it. Really. Hey, it's all pink on the inside, right? But there was this one girl, though . . .

Abby was somethin' special. She was the one that made me think maybe I really was gonna have the wife and the house in the 'burbs and the dog in the yard and well, the whole nine, y'know? Straighten me out. And kids. She was crazy about kids. Said she wanted to have a whole army of 'em runnin' around. She painted a sweet picture in my head. She gave me a way out and I took it. I played the part. Blew two month's pay on a ring, and we got engaged.

Got the family off my back, too . . . the questions stopped, and Pops started pattin' me on the back all the time, like I scored the winning touchdown in the Friday night high school football game. I knew what it all meant, and it felt good, like we were all on the same side now.

When Abby got pregnant, they acted like I was a returning war hero. They didn't care we weren't married yet. Jesus, you'd think I discovered the cure for cancer! And I was gonna

be—a dad! So Abby wants to set a date and seal the deal, b
suddenly I'm realizin' I'm not as in a hurry as she is about this
but she keeps naggin' and naggin' about it, how she doesn't
want our baby to be born a bastard and where the hell was I
again last night and why didn't I call her up and Christ! I'm
suffocating!

I grab my jacket and head down to the local spot. After I
do a few shots, I can breathe again . . . I'm feeling good,
relaxed now, and then there's a nod and a grin from across the
bar, and I'm walking to the back room and in a second I'm in
his mouth and his stubble feels so good on my skin, and I'm
melting into him and my eyes are rolling back in my head and
then POW!

I'm gettin' pummeled with angry, clenched fists and the
air is full of her rage, screaming, shrieking "You fucking faggot
how could you do this to us?" and then she pukes all over me
as I'm trying to zip myself up and how the hell was I supposed
to know she followed me there? I'm trying to calm her down
but she won't and she falls to her knees, howling in pain and
clutching at her belly and an ambulance comes and I'm scared
and they take her off but I stay behind . . .

I tried to call her, but I never saw her again. My folks told
me she had a miscarriage. That's the last time they spoke to
me. It's so black and white for them. Life's on automatic . . .
all the mile markers are set along the way, like a well-worn
path that you just get on and go. Society roots for you. Settle
down and get married, buy a house, make some babies, and
get old. Fuck that! I do love kids. Maybe someday.

There is a silence as SON *stands in front of everyone, finding the right words to say.*

SON: The best I can do right now is to think of three things and the day I was born. An hourglass. A rock. A Father's Day card. And the day I was born.

When an hourglass bursts from the weight of new-formed gravel, it means that a man is born and will continue to grow.

Sand in an hourglass is contained, following orders from the forces that hold it and turn it and shake it. The sand is always there, moving, but never growing. Nothing can reach inside of it or shape it or touch it. Time and experience in a vacuum, trapped in a box, never collecting anything, never becoming bigger, never casting a shadow. An aquarium of kinetic nothing, aspiring and hoping to be something more.

It takes millions of years for a grain of sand to become a piece of gravel. Through time and trial, sand collects things and becomes bigger. It weathers the tides and the rains and the wind, always getting bigger as it stays true to itself—a larger form of itself all the time growing. Sand. Silt. Sediment. A pebble. A rock. A rock. That's what we always called my father. A rock.

Last Father's Day, I got him a card. I took time to choose the right one. I looked through the wall of Father's Day cards, opening and reading each one, hoping to find the right words. What caught my attention most was a black-and-white photo of a grown man and a young boy, probably age four. The age when your dad feels as big as he looks. The man and boy were walking forward, the man in front of the boy, with their backs turned to the viewer—as if they were walking towards the inside of the card, which said—"thanks for letting me walk in your shadow. I love you." Shortly after reading this Father's Day card, the shapely glass walls around me broke open, making a mess of silken sand and shattered shards and the tears, like now, just flowed. (*Takes a moment to compose himself.*)

I remember now that in my early twenties I started collecting rocks. Not too many. Just a few at a time. I'd lay them on the windowsills of the various vagabond dwellings I've lived in over the years. It seems clear to me now what I've been doing: Despite our distance, I guess I always wanted my father to be near me. To look in on me to see how I was doing. I wanted his guidance, his acceptance, his company.

Starting tomorrow, I'll begin to give these rocks away. I'll give them away as gifts, because I know I don't need them anymore. On this day, I know now that my father's always been with me, waiting for me to break through and to become something bigger.

A rock casts a large shadow. Thank you for letting me walk in it and teaching me to cast my own. I love you.

Men of His Generation

EUGENE STICKLAND

LUKE stands in a single spotlight. He is in his early 40's, very handsome, dressed in a dark suit, white shirt, conservative tie.

LUKE: Of my father, my mother used to say, "Men of his generation." And then make one of those tisking, clucking sounds that mothers used to make, and go back to the task at hand. They were, the men of my father's generation, inheritors of the world, as they understood it, and they moved through the world with a nonchalance, verging at times on arrogance, that you seldom see today. To us, looking back, they were dinosaurs, an extinct species now, that we can't really hope to understand from the few clues they left to us. All we know is that once they ruled the world, but the world they ruled has changed, irrevocably, for better or for worse.

Growing up, I observed my father, and learned from him, and as a result, there are times when I feel out of step with the world around me. For example, my father never dabbled in what has become the national pastime for men of my generation—home improvements. Repairs. Renovation. Restoration. Whatever. He had no time for it. No interest in it. And I would go so far as to say, a certain dignity about him that kept him from even considering doing it himself. He subscribed to a rather simple but effective philosophy of trickle-down economics for our neighborhood—that being, if there was need for a repair, then the logical course of events was to call in a tradesman to do the job, and pay him for his troubles, thereby propping up the local economy.

When something went wrong, when something needed fixing, my father would stand, smoking his pipe, contemplating the broken window, or the overflowing toilet, and eventually reach not for the putty knife, or the plunger, but for the telephone. He would then beseech the man on the other end to drop by for a cup of coffee, or a drink if it were later in the day, and if it wasn't too much trouble, maybe he could have a look at the toilet that was threatening to flood the second floor of our house? Along with the usual assortment of aunts and uncles and friends of the family, our circle included Austin the carpenter, Norm the plumber, and even a strange little man named Paul, the glazier, who somehow eked out a living repairing the broken window panes in our neighborhood. There were a lot of boys around, and we played a lot of baseball. Paul survived.

What I have inherited from my father, I suppose, beyond the obvious, is a certain disdain for the kind of man who does things for himself. Who fixes things for himself. I do not saw. I do not hammer. I have never routed. I refuse to plumb. And I shudder when I drive by a Home Depot on a Saturday morning and see those poor lost souls loading their supplies into their vans, or their station wagons. And I wonder why their own fathers failed to teach them the valuable lessons my own father taught me. Or was it that these men of my generation failed to learn the often subtle but infinitely practical lessons derived from the wisdom of the men of his generation . . . ?

(*He leaves.*)

Last Farewell

MICHEL WALLERSTEIN

MARK, *a dark-haired man in his early twenties is standing, center stage, a few feet away from an open casket. His hands are clasped in front of him, in "praying position." What we hear are his thoughts. Mark never looks straight at the coffin in front of him.*

MARK: I can't believe the rabbi just opened the casket. What did he say? Something about our last chance to ask for forgiveness? Shit, I wasn't paying attention . . . Why is mom staring at him like that? I don't want to look at him. I know he's my father. Well, was. But I'm not going to look inside that coffin. No way . . . I'll pretend. That's right. I'll pretend to look at him, but I'll look at the wall . . . Poor mom, must be hard for her to realize that this is all that's left of the man she's lived with for almost thirty years. The coffin looks so small, I thought dad was taller. Oh my God, she just touched his cheek. God! I know he's my father, but still, mom just touched a dead man's cheek. Caressed him, like he was just sleeping! (*Calming down.*)

It doesn't seem to bother her. I guess she sees dead bodies all the time being a nurse and all. (*Takes a step forward.*)

My sister looks good. She made an effort for once. Great, now she's also staring. She probably figures if mom can stare at him for like a minute, she'd better stare for a minute and a half. These two are so competitive, it's pathetic. Well I don't care, I won't look at him. Oh great! Now she's caressing his cheek too. Shit. Is this like a Jewish custom I never heard of, or something? No one touched uncle Marty when he died, did they? Well, I'm sorry, but I'm not touching a dead man's cheek and that's final. Hell, I never touched dad while he was alive, why should I do it now? If they ask, I'll just say that Dad was not the touchy feely type. (*Takes another step forward.*)

I don't know why Aunt Debbie is in front of me. Isn't a son like, more important than a sister? Jesus, look at her. Didn't anyone tell her this was a funeral and not a bar mitzvah? She'd better not lean over the coffin like that, her tits are going to fall out. I bet she'll touch his cheek too. Big drama queen like her—she wouldn't miss that opportunity for the world—she'll tell everyone that she felt his energy when she touched him; that his soul went through her or some crap like that. There you go, I knew it. Maybe I should quick ask the rabbi, if the Bible says anything about cheek touching. Jesus, she's not letting go, is she? Fuck, I'm next. (*Suddenly very solemn, takes a step forward; takes a deep breath, looks straight ahead of him.*)

Hi . . . Sorry, I can't look at you, but you understand . . . The rabbi says we should ask for your forgiveness now and I'm sure there are plenty of things I've said or done to you that I'm sorry for. But right now, I don't know what I'm feeling, so I don't know what I should apologize for . . . (*Lowers his eyes and actually stares at his dead father.*)

I don't know what to say to you. Let's face it, we never had much to say to each other. Maybe that was our problem . . . You would come to my room—usually when I was working on my music—and announce solemnly that we needed to have a talk and to meet you in the living room. By the time I'd get there, you'd be reading your paper and when I'd ask what you wanted to talk about, you'd always say: "I don't remember now." . . . But you loved us. I know you did. And I . . . I loved you too? I think. Fuck, I don't know. Can you live with that? I mean, well you know what I mean. (*Getting angry.*)

I hope you weren't expecting tears from me, because those aren't coming . . . Look, I don't even know if I miss you yet. I mean, you weren't exactly an overwhelming presence in my life . . . Look, I don't know what I'm feeling, and maybe that's better, because I'm sick of this emptiness in the pit of my stomach. Or maybe it's my heart, I was never good at anatomy. But I don't want to feel it anymore. And I don't want to feel lost, like I don't belong on this Godless planet of ours. And I don't want to be afraid that maybe, just maybe, this whole "be happy you're alive" and "be thankful for your health" crap is just . . . crap and that in fact, as I've always suspected it, life isn't such a great gift after all, but just a tedious and useless journey . . . So, because I don't want to feel any of these things, I've gone numb inside. Numb's good. It's colorless, odorless, painless. I like it. I think. After all, I learned from the best. (*Smiles sadly, then slowly lifts his right hand and cups his father's cheek. After a beat, he exits.*)

Sleeping, Son

MICHAEL WRIGHT

NICK, in his young son's room, late at night. He moves as the words move him.

Little boy, if you knew how I love to watch you sleep . . .

I need to say this to you, now, and then I need to live it, need you to hold me to it, fierce as only you can be in your nine-year-old outlaw way.

I want you to be better than me.

I know, I know, this is what fathers say to sons, but I don't mean it like have a better job or anything like that.

I mean, live more truly.

More truly than me.

I realize that you got stuff from me that just came with the deal: my big nose might show up on your face any day now; you already got the cheekbones. That stuff I know you can work with; it's just genes, DNA, luck of the draw.

But what I fear is that there are other genes, like my anger or secrecy, that are in you.

And I don't know how to keep them from you, from poisoning you like they've poisoned me in my life.

Toxic, stupid, blind . . .

Did I get them from my father? I know I watched him burn in anger day after day, unhappy with his life, mad enough to run right over the cord on the electric lawnmower in sheer driven rage at having to mow the "god-damned lawn." And I know he had secrets, just like I do.

I think all men have secrets. I think we're driven to it. Can't be a crybaby, can't be silly around "real" men—unless you're drunk, of course—can't be creative when you're supposed to be a sports freak or a crotch-hoisting, sneering tough guy.

Can't, finally, *be*.

But those are just one kind of secret. I mean something else, I mean the kind of secrets that we hide even from ourselves. Like what we dream of for two seconds and then bury for fear we might actually live out that dream. The kind of deep, buried, locked-down wish that visits in the night and makes you want to scream your guts out for wanting it, dying from the scraped-out hunger to hope.

For anything.

For one moment of simple, true, clear, breathable . . . peace.

Something my father never found . . .

It's a spiral, little boy: Secrets lead to lying, lying to anger, anger to secrets, the wheel spins, and pretty soon you're just a locked-up heap of flesh, impenetrable and walled-in, a pointless, moronic and blinded animal, like some macho idiot that's gotten out of the funhouse car and can't find his way through the maze.

And here comes the screaming skeleton.

And that's where I don't want you to end up.

Sometimes I hate it so much, I fear it so much for your life that I want to kill it in me, like I could just cut it out of my chest and be rid of it, throw it in a dumpster.

But that's what I saw one day: rage can't kill off rage. No. It's only food, then—fuel: alcohol tossed on flames.

So I try this instead, my sweet boy. I talk to you while you sleep. I sit on your floor and I try to meditate and quell the fire. That's why I took that class, to end the spiral if I can, to learn how to meditate on what they call the mind poisons. And, phew, I've got all three—anger, greed, delusion—big time.

But you know what? Seeing them made them real to me.

And I'm hoping I can be real for you, then.

Because maybe it's not in the genes, but it sure is in the life. All the stuff I watched my father do, all the times he lashed out and hit me with words and with his hands? That's what he taught me about being a man.

And that's the biggest lie.

And I won't tell you the same lies; I swear to every god there is I won't—not by what I do or think or act. No.

I want all that to end with me.

I want all that to end with me.

That's my mantra, son; for you.

And it's the secret, too, the one I wanted to touch for so long, and I just got it tonight, in this clear little flash.

The secret, little man; so simple: I'm not like that—like him—and I don't have to be like that—and neither do you.

So I want all that to end.

With me.

And tomorrow I'll say this to you in the light. Good night.

The Man Dance

Damn, it's all gains and losses, ain't it, bro? Grew pubic hair and thought I was a real man . . . until I lost that shit on my head. Then felt half a man . . . until I grew grey and was reduced to a third. Then it just fell out altogether and I felt a fifth . . . of a man.

Was friggin' King of the World when that 401K rose quicker than my dick ever could. Felt lower than Satan's ballsack in Hell when the market dropped out and my precious, precarious 401K shriveled up and died a painful, choking, longing for a last-breath death.

Think I'd be used to that one step forward, twelve steps back; but I was never one for dancing, prancing, or posing. But it's the Man Dance, and I'm here 'till the song ends.

Crowed like a rooster when she walked into my life. Could be heard for miles and miles cock-oh-cock-a-doodle-doing. And the only thing that matched that sound was my sob when she left, or was taken away from me. Actually, that's not true. I cried real loud when *he* left, because what the hell was I doing with a he anyway. Or even louder, when the second she took out. Or the third he went away. Or the first they dissolved into nothing.

One step forward, twelve steps back. The Man Dance. Doesn't matter who you dance with, bro, or where you do the dance (which reminds me, finally got that goddamn good job and the fuckin' company is under federal investigation for playing with its bottom line numbers), it feels like . . . gains and losses; stock-market positions working my soul's last nerve.

How to Quit Properly

NATE EPPLER

EMPLOYEE: No. You know what? I think—Yeah. I have something to say. If, of course, you fine gentlemen will permit me. No objections? No? No? Excellent. Mr. Rosenthal. Mr. Forbes. Mr. Vannick. May I congratulate the three of you on being uncompromisingly shortsighted and remarkably bald. Oh, please don't get up. I've hardly begun.

After working for your company for two short years, I have found that what I learned in my first two short days is the ultimate truth of your company. You value nothing. Your company values nothing. All of this, all of this, your margins and memos and faxes and directives? All of it is, pardon my French, absolute motherfucking bullshit. All of it is nothing. Your bottom line? Nothing. Your holdings? Nonexistent. As are, I might add, your petty little reasons for terminating me. Nothing. Your company is an overvalued balloon filled with nothing but hot, stinking air. All you seem to value is you.

And not even you as a team. You individually. From the bottom of the mailroom all the way up to you three geniuses. Everybody making sure that their pockets are thoroughly lined. So I guess it's not like you have nothing at all. You have money. And you have a few short years left before you become completely outdated. Before you are replaced by the new model. Before retirement vapor-locks your ass to a leather chair and not-so-little grandchildren pull on your loose flesh until money pops out.

And those years really are the golden years, aren't they? Blissful retirement years punctuated by painful chemotherapy treatments and soothing rounds of golf. Years spent watching your prostate like a hawk and praying tomorrow isn't the day you finally break your hip. Which will happen closer to sooner than to later, gentlemen. And then, after that . . . Well, shit, boys, you'll be dead. I bet you can hardly wait.

Think of all the things you have to look forward to. So, yeah, I'd be pissed at me too. I'm younger, I'm smarter, I'm faster, I can still fuck, and I don't wear dark blue. And when retirement does show up to swallow you whole, I'll be there. Fucking your granddaughter and laughing my ass off at your inevitable stockpile of adult diapers. And we'll all look back on today and have a good laugh. Because, hey, job termination happens every day, right? I'll be back on my feet in no time.

This is just the way things go. And besides, it doesn't really matter. Eventually I'll get your jobs anyway. And I'll be the one firing the young asshole who doesn't know who he's talking to. And he'll learn from me exactly what I learned from you. I am the only thing that matters. A word of advice, gentlemen. It's time to stop treating this world like it's yours. You're borrowing it from me. And I will be back to collect. My office will be cleaned out by five.

Lunch

JASON T. GARRETT

A twenty-something male epiphanizes about love.

TWENTY-SOMETHING: The happiest day of my life? That was the day Vinnie stopped by just to see if I got my lunch.

Y'see, Vinnie and me, we were kind of serious. We'd only been datin' about three months, but everything 'til then had been fireworks—y'know, romantic evenings, stupid road trips, all-night talks about the future. And then, two days ago, Vinnie stops in at work just to see if I got my lunch. And I smile and I say yeah and my friend Elise at the counter is kinda giggling and I say I'll see ya tonight? with that kinda lift at the end that's sort of a half-question/half-confirmation thing? And Vinnie just winks and leaves.

And as soon as that door shuts, I start bawling. Elise is asking what's wrong and do I need a tissue and I say, no, everything's fine. And she says what is it, please tell me, you're keeping something from me, and I say, it's just . . . he's . . . Vinnie's thinking about me in an everyday way, you know? In a real, grounded, I'm-not-going-anywhere way. He doesn't need big moments, he doesn't need dinner by candlelight, he just . . . he just wants to know if I got my lunch. That's what he cares about, that's where he is, that's what my Vinnie wants to know. It's that moment of Ohmigod, I'm gonna wake up next to you grinning for the next 50 years.

So, on the way home, I pick up some flowers, and of course I go overboard. And I'm almost to the door when I think, no, he doesn't want all this, he doesn't *need* overboard. So I throw away everything except one little rose—which I put in my teeth for effect—and as I walk through that door, I think: I had the guts to make us romantic, but Vinnie had the guts to make us real.

Yeah, Vinnie, I got my lunch. I got my lunch and then some.

In the Arboretum

JON HALLER

MASON stands looking out. There is a handkerchief wrapped around his knuckles.

MASON: Don't close the door. Listen. You were right. You asked me to do nothing and I should have listened. See, he was playing pool tonight at the Turf when I went to get my paycheck. He came over and I couldn't stop it. This need. A confession. That's all I wanted from him. An apology. I don't know. Something. You deserve something. He said game of eight ball, I said fuck yeah.

I break and like that, he starts cracking jokes. Coke habits in Amish communities. Shit like that. And what's weird is I'm enjoying it. Laughing with him. Like nothing happened. Like I forget. What he did to you. I get so confused. Who is this guy, you know. Who the fuck is he. So I ask him. Flat out. Did you do it? What Stace said. In the arboretum two nights ago. Did you rape her?

He's leaning in to take a shot. Down to the eight ball in the far pocket. You could whisper that ball in. He looks at me and says, Mason, I never even been to the arboretum. And then he does this thing. Right before he leans in to finish the game, he wipes his mouth. Like this. I've never seen him do that. He plays a straight game every time. Chalk up, lean in, sink the shot. Ritual. But this time. Wipes his mouth, shoots, and scratches. He never scratches, Stace.

So I know. Everything you said. All of it was right. Sick thing is I start seeing it. Everything you described. Him over you. His hand on your throat. His thumbs making those bruises on your jaw. And you. Looking out. Into the arboretum. At all those trees. Like you said. Leaning in. Like an audience. Like they were watching. But not doing anything. Well, I start feeling like those trees. The way I was seeing it all. 'Cause I'm doing nothing too. He's right there in front of me and I'm doing nothing. So I change. For you. For me. I—look at my hand, Stace. That's from his teeth. I pick up the eight ball. He's smiling when I come at him. His smile. So white. It's. No. A grin. He's grinning. I can't. Blink. It's so good. When I smash into him. Eight ball into his mouth. His grin. Over and over. Like this. My hand in his mouth. All those teeth. Pcccch.

I took his smile. I took it. Tell me that's okay.

'Lac

VISHAKAN JEYAKUMAR

Baby, let me explain before you go and do somethin' crazy . . .
Just calm down now . . . take a couple of breaths . . . that's
right, breathe . . . No, no! Don't go pickin' up that fryin' pan!
Baby, please! Give me a chance to explain!

That's right . . . I can explain . . . that's right . . . Baby, you
know I work hard . . . been workin' hard all my life. Okay, so
it ain't the backbreakin' kind of work my daddy had, but baby,
it's still work . . . I mean, it's tough makin' sure I get the right
price at the right time. You put most fools out there on the
floor and they break under pressure. But not me, baby. Hell,
no. I'm cool. Baby, you know I'm cool.

So about the Escalade—don't go doin' nothin' crazy
now—I know it's not what we agreed on, but, baby, just hear
me out it. It was a magnetic attraction drawin' me in, you
know. Like a cosmic force or some shit. I'm tellin' you, baby, I
was checkin' out all the lame-ass cars when . . .

Baby, please! Put the fryin' pan down! At least let me
finish before you start swingin'! You're scarin' me, baby. Okay
. . . easy . . . that's it . . . let me finish. The salesman was
shootin' his mouth off about the Volvo being the safest, the
Oldsmobile being the best value, blah, blah, blah, when all of
a sudden this thing, this beautiful, beautiful thing, caught the
corner of my eye. You should've seen her, baby. She was black
. . . and beautiful—just like you. When I saw her, I knew I
had to have her. It was like the day I met you.

Ease up on the fryin' pan now, baby . . . the fryin' pan . . .
Look, I know what we talked about. I know, the price of gas,

the space . . . And I'm not sayin' your Honda Civic ain't cool. Hey, it's cool it can get 40 miles to the gallon. It's cool you can park it anywhere you want. And I know what some people think. Gettin' somethin' that big is compensatin' for not havin' much of somethin' else. But, shit, that ain't true. Baby, you sure as hell know that ain't true.

I don't understand why you makin' such a big deal out of this? (*Shock.*) No, baby!!! (*Dodges swing.*) Baby, wait!! I ain't finished explainin'! Please! (*Backs away.*) That's right. Let me finish. (*Beat, as he thinks quickly.*)

Baby, did you know I'm buyin' into history? (*Unsure.*) Uh huh. That's right. Gettin' this truck is my way of givin' props to cats before me. Even back in the day cats used to holler about Cadillacs. You remember them old school cats talkin' about their Broughams and Coupe DeVilles? Now we got all these new school "dawgs" talkin' 'bout that thing sittin' out in the driveway. Escalade is the way of the future, baby. (*Nervous.*) Them 22-inch rims? They were optional. But I had to get them you know. It's a hip-hop thing—you wouldn't understand. (*Scared.*) No, no, I didn't mean it like that! It's just that Celine Dion ain't gonna be singin' 'bout no Escalade sittin' on dubs, you know what I'm sayin'? (*Sulking.*)

Kevin got himself a new Dodge Ram! That fool lives in Midtown and he got himself a pick-up truck! I mean at least I gotta cross the bridge. I need that height, baby. I need the off-road capabilities . . . to navigate that jungle out there, you know. The concrete jungle, that's what I'm talkin' 'bout. (*Beat—thinking.*) Plus we can go campin'. Yeah. That's right. I forget to mention she's an all-terrain vehicle? (*More confident.*) Oh hell, yeah. You can drive her over two, three feet of snow and she'll still make ground. We can go out to the mountains—just the two of us—stay for a weekend, drive around, see the trees and thangs.

No need for the fryin' pan now, right? (*Relieved.*) You're my baby. Always did understand me. I knew you would. (*Confident.*)

Baby, I got me a Cadillac Escalade. You'll be able to spot me in a crowd. Volvos and Oldsmobiles will move the hell out my way if I gotta go somewhere fast. And only time I'll have to go somewhere fast . . . is when I have to see you.

Let's go for a drive right now. It'll just be you and me . . . Cruisin' in my 'lac.

Down for the Count

KIPP KOENIG

The Present. Airport. BERT, *30s, describes to a crowd of friends how he met his wife.*

BERT: Oh, I remember the first time I saw her. She was passed out on the floor. Not as in drunk at a college party. It was Armstrong's department store.

I was there for socks. Came around a corner of a sock aisle and—whammo—sleeping beauty, down for the count. That's what I thought. What a beauty. Right there on the floor in front of me. Her hair, this thick gorgeous hair, got twisted and caught up in an abandoned shoe rack and wrapped around her nose and it went up and down when she would breathe. See, Natalie's hair is to me what wings must be to an angel. And she was kind of snoring—just a little. A cute little poppy kindofa "snsnnsnsnsnsns." And well, obviously, I got all caught up in this and then it occurred to me—people don't normally, you know, sleep in the men's shoe department. Especially not women.

And the place was deserted—not a soul. You know—department stores. It was late on a Tuesday, close to closing. You can never get a salesperson in the shoe department, anyway, much less one that knows CPR. But she didn't need CPR. She was asleep. I thought about getting some sheets and a pillow from the bedding department—which was not 20 steps away—when she started to come to. Real groggy. Like she'd been there for hours.

"Where am I?" "The third floor at Armstrong's. You, uh, it looks like you were taking a nap." She looked at me like I was nuts, but, well, she was the one on the floor. Then somehow, naturally almost, like God put the thought in me, I knelt down and offered her my hand. It's comforting to know that deep down inside us men there are these unshakable instincts of chivalry. 'Cause she took my hand, again quite naturally, and then paused.

What a pause. Part of me is still back there—still in it—still looking down at those enormous limpid pools. And then, of course, there was the requisite swelling feeling inside—you know, with heat, when you feel like a big piece of plumbing down in your chest just burst and buckets a stuff are filling up your rib cage like a bathtub. And everything is speeding up and stopping at the same time. Well, you know what I mean. Hey, I just came for socks. I figure, you get maybe two or three of those pauses in your life, and one you're virtually guaranteed to get at the very end of your life. But here's the thing. When that happens, you always wonder if what's happening to you is happening to the other person. And of course your voice cracks and you haven't taken a breath in five minutes, so immediately an otherwise normal situation—except for the sleeping on the floor part—becomes quite embarrassing.

I was so out of breath I had to pause again just so I could help her up. Come to think of it, I don't remember us actually saying a lot. But I still hadn't found my socks and well, she kind of followed me around—you know, like some kind of lost baby duck. So the story is, the reason she was asleep, she has this problem with passing out whenever she experiences even remotely intense physical pain. Turns out she's a real klutz too. Bad combination. Always passing out in the strangest places whenever she bangs a knee or stubs a toe. So that's my lost baby duck—my Natalie—followed me all the way to the altar about two years later. God, I love my wife.

The Crafty Baboon

CARLOS MURILLO

ANONYMOUS: Did you catch that documentary they showed
on Discovery Channel? *Baboon Warriors of the Serengeti?*
Man . . .
It was *fucked*
up.
I saw it last Thursday night and I can't get the fucking thing
out of my head. It was incredible, the whole thing was just
unb . . . *lie*vable.
I mean those little fuckers are *mean.*
There was this *one* part.
And this, this is the part that really *stuck* with me
the part I can't extricate from my craw I mean
Jesus . . .
They were talking about this *thing*
this whole *phenomenon* that happens on planet baboon
this whole *phenomenon* of a certain *kind* of baboon they call
The *Crafty* Baboon see:
Baboons have a whole tribal hierarchy thing going
the alpha males hunt for food and fight the wars
beta males make this perimeter around camp keeping watch
so
the *fe*males staying at home can rear little future alphas in
peace.
End of the day
Alphas come home from the hunt
and being all tired, sweaty and riled up from the hard work
naturally

they're in the mood to *get* some
a kind of payment or reward or whatever
for busting their asses out in the jungle all day.
Simple.
But *then*
there's this *other* kind a baboon
The *Crafty* Baboon.
He's like the third- or fourth-string male
the dead weight
the useless one
the social critic that can't keep his mouth shut
criticizes and complains about everything, the living arrange-
ments, the food, the breakdown of the democratic process,
corrects the other baboons' use of grammar, talks a lot of bullshit. *But*: the Crafty Baboon doesn't have the will, skill,
courage or prestige to *do* anything about it, he can only talk
up a storm, raise hell until one of the alphas gets sick of his
yabber and knocks 'em one upside the head.
But let me tell you, for all his lack of will and skill, the little
fucker's got a sex drive like you wouldn't believe, which of
course is a problem cause all the good women are already spoken for by one of the alphas in the tribe, but the little fucker's
got to get off somehow so:

What he does—
and *this*.
is.
fascinating—
What he *does*—
is he *waits*.
At the crack of dawn
while the baboon kids are still asleep
and while the females are packin' up lunchboxes for the
alphas' hunt
The Crafty Baboon sleeps with one eye open
watching the whole thing,

waiting. . . .
He watches the "good-bye-have-a-nice-day-at-work" kisses,
he watches the alphas march off one by one into the jungle
he watches the females on the porch, wearing their aprons
and waving their goodbyes
you'd think it was the fuckin' Brady Bunch
And the horny little fucker lies in wait like that
til he sees the last purple-assed alpha
disappear through the trees.
Which is his *cue.*
His eyes pop wide open,
he springs up to his hind legs
and the little fucker's up and at 'em.
Heart beating like he's on crack.
Can't tell if he's grining or grimacing
but either way he's so worked up
it looks like his face is about to shatter into a thousand shards.
And he starts chanting to himself
I'M THE MILKMAN
I'M THE PLUMBER
I'M THE PIZZA BOY
I'M THE UPS GUY
I'M THE CABLE GUY
and one by one he starts fucking everything in sight
all those unattainable, spoken-for alpha females
Yeah, he fucks everything in sight *but*
he can't *enjoy* it cause . . .
the *alphas* might come home
unannounced any second
and if one of the alphas *caught* him. . . .

whhheyyll.

So while he's bouncing up and down like a lunatic pogo stick
he keeps looking over his shoulder
can't concentrate

can't savor the moment
doesn't notice the "are-you-done-yet" look on the chick's face
the tiniest rustling of leaves sets off a paranoia in him
that'd make Jim Jones envious.
That's how he spends his whole day, day after day:
Paranoid, sweating, a jangle of nerves
heart beat away from having a coronary,
fucking everything in sight
but incapable of taking an ounce of pleasure in it.
Ohhh . . .
The footage in the documentary was un . . . b . . . *lie*vable.
And
you don't even want to *know*
what happens when the Crafty Baboon gets caught in the act.

I never knew flesh and fur could be torn up like paper.

Panthers, Police, and Baby Mamas

MALCOM PELLES

MARIO, late 20s, M. African American, wears jeans and T-shirt.

SETTING: Washington, DC, 1969. On an apartment building stoop as Caroline (Mario's ex-girlfriend) is coming home from work. He tries to block Caroline's path as she tries to enter her building.

MARIO: Caroline, I need to see my daughter. I know that I agreed to keep my distance, but I need to see her. I told myself I'd give you time to adjust to shit, but she's just starting to talk and listen and she needs her father to rap to. Just for a few minutes—I'll hit the bricks in just a half an hour. What you say?

I've been real cool, but this you-can't-see-Sharon foolishness has got to stop—I'm not letting you up this stoop until you listen to me—until you get some damn sense in your head. You treat me like I'm some kind of animal . . . You tell Sharon I'm an animal, don't you? I'm sure you don't tell her the truth—that the Black Panther Party is in the forefront of re-molding how things go down in this country. I bet you don't tell her that you were in the streets with us. (*He studies her closely.*)

You do think I'm some kind of an ox? That I don't have feelings. How else can I get by—I must be an ox. How could I stand pigs pulling me over to search my car on the way to First Baptist to make pancakes for the kids, detaining me when I'm on my way to and from work, throwing all kinds of guns in my face while I'm out selling papers? How can I go through all that and still have enough steam to go into the Party office at night to actually do some work? I can't be human—a human won't put himself through that. Put his children through that. They would have left the Party like you did.

I haven't turned into no animal. I am still the same dude that likes fried catfish and cheese grits; I still like the Gladys Knight version of "I Heard It Through the Grapevine" over the Marvin Gaye one; and I'm still a John Wayne nut—no matter how counterrevolutionary it is.

I do what I do because I believe in the righteousness of the struggle. I know that in forty years you won't even be able to recognize this country it'll be so changed. It ain't just us that's in the trenches, right? White kids with their long manes and dirty, naked feet are out there protesting Vietnam, across the country college groups are issuing demands to their administrations; gang members who used to peddle reefer are peddling Red Books now.

And this country—it's about to bust at the seams, right? They losing the war; folks is in the streets by the tens of thousands; and in '68—this time last year—all the big cities was on fire. Things just can't go on being like they've been. This is our chance to snatch hold of the moment—it's now or never, right? And I'm a part of that. I'm a revolutionary. I'm a breakfast-program sausage-cooking, assault-rifle cleaning, Chairman Mao quoting, poetry-writing, freedom-fighting motherfucker. And my daughter has a right to see me . . . Please let me see her. (*A pause.*)

Pigs shot up our office. Two nights ago. It looks like a mini-Vietnam happened. The sandbags we had in place didn't do nothing. Windows are shattered. The doors are splintered and hanging on their hinges. Holes the size of silver dollars are in the walls. The poster of Huey has a hole in his face. Malcolm X has a hole through his stomach. They want us out of DC.

We had a meeting. We're going back. Tomorrow—we're opening the office up again. We've fought too hard to let it go. I think about the attack and nobody was in the office, but there could have been. Maybe next time somebody will be. Maybe a political education meeting will be happening. Maybe women and children will be there . . . I could be there. Maybe next time I'll get a hole in my face.

Caroline, I'm scared. I'm scared and I just want to see my little girl. If I didn't get a chance to see her and something were to happen—Listen, I'll only be a half an hour. Then I'll hit the bricks—I swear.

Scrap

ARZHANG PEZHMAN

KID: It rained that morning. Heavy night the night before, so, bleary-eyed I drove through the grey to pick her up. I've just passed my test, Dad left me the car in his will, and how I love it. I love driving, you know? Rolling up a small spliff, getting a bit stoned and cruising around listening to banging tunes! I'd saved up a little cash, summer job, wanted to fit a hardcore stereo as soon as I could but . . . today was going to cost. Pulling up to her house, blown speakers crackling at max volume, I hit the horn. She comes out. Lives in a nice area, nice house. A face peers at me from one of the top windows, must be her mum, don't really know her family. She gets in and my tyres squeal as I accelerate away. Love it.

She looks good, always looks good. I look like shit, but we don't talk about that. We don't talk about ourselves. Instead we talk about other people at college. Who's fucking who, who's fucking who behind whose back, and who's not fucking at all. And never will. We have a laugh. I have to keep stopping and asking her for directions because she's the one that knows the way.

We drive down a narrow street with tall trees, green and leafy. The place is close. As we get near I notice a group of people huddled under umbrellas, standing at the bottom of the driveway. This is the place. Turning sharply, screeching up the path, a few of the faces turn to look at us. Pale, blank, like death. (*Lights a cigarette.*) Gives me the creeps.

We park, and smoke a cigarette before going in. God, how I love smoking. Only been doing it for a couple of years. I

135

used to be a right fat bastard, used to eat loads of sweets, and then I started smoking. Lost loads of weight, but I still like sweets. I remember my first cigarette, no coughing or being sick, the smoke just slipped down easy. I'm glad she smokes. We just sit there, silently smoking.

At reception they send us upstairs, narrow, tall steps that get difficult as they go around corners. At the top there's a waiting room, another couple, older than us. We sit and wait. Eventually a nurse comes out of a side door. Small, old, shrivelled like a prune. She has an accent, Polish I think. Calls the patients 'my little von,' which is funny seeing as my girlfriend's almost six feet tall. They both disappear into the side room. I sit and wait, just me and the other couple. The woman has tears in her eyes, the man stares at me sternly. What's his fucking problem?

When they come out, the nurse ushers us back down the stairs. A bigger waiting room, more couples, more our age, more tears. My girlfriend doesn't cry, we just sit and hold hands until it's her turn.

Then it's her turn and she goes. (*Reclines.*) And I sit and wait and wait and wait and . . . (*Jolts.*) I'm woken by a screaming child. Fuck, I hate crying kids. First the long shrieks . . . (*Imitates.*) Then the short, broken wailing . . . (*Imitates.*) Then the sharp intakes of breath across a quivering bottom lip. (*Imitates.*) So forced and . . . false! And what the fuck is a *baby* doing here anyway! I have to get out of here. (*He yawns/stretches/lights up a cigarette.*)

Outside the air's cold but not fresh. I walk down the driveway looking up, watching the rain fall into my eyes, when I hear it, very quiet, but . . . chanting? I edge down the path and it grows louder. It's the group we saw when we came in. Christians . . . pro-life Christians . . . and they're chanting . . . the Lord's Prayer. Praying . . . praying for the unborn. (*Pause.*) My heart fills with rage. I want to smash all their faces in. I want to tell them about the real world, the single mums, single dads. The starving children, unwanted. I want to tell them about my father . . . but I don't. I don't do any of these things. I just go back inside.

She's waiting for me. She's done. (*Pause.*) In the car, she tells me she came around after the operation in a room full of sobbing girls. She tells me she got up and started to put her clothes on almost immediately, the nurse tried to stop her but she was out the door. That's my girl. I give her a cigarette and we smoke.

I ask her if she wants to go and see a film next week. Yeah, she says, and gives me a lollipop the nurse gave her. She doesn't like sweets. I unwrap it and pop it in my mouth. Mm. (*Drags off his cigarette.*) Sweet.

Vinnie G

RICHARD STOCKTON RAND

Frankie, Frank, Frank, you, you, you, we don't see one another anymore. I know, business, tell me about it. But, it's yours now, Frankie, am I right? The bakery. And it's the best, Frankie, the best in Brooklyn. And the cannoli. No one can touch your cannoli. You done good with the place. Antonio would be proud. That's why I'm having a hard time understanding this, this singing business.

To give up the bakery for something like, like that, Frank, I don't know. Because I'll tell you, Frank, I've seen fortunes in the gutter on sure things like—like this. Wait, wait, Frank! What, I don't have faith!? Frank, Frank, who fronted you the money for the new ovens and the big neon sign? Ahhh! It comes back now. So calm down, you crazy person, you, and explain to me what it is you hope to achieve with this plan.

You see, to me, Frank, when I think of singers, I think Sinatra, Tony Bennett. But that was a different era. Frank, I know you can sing. You got talent. We saw it at Cecile's wedding. What a voice! But to give up the bakery, maybe lose everything. Now, I believe in you Frank, I believe in this dream of yours. And not to discourage you, Frank, no, 'cause I care about you. Know that, Frank, but know also that it's a crapshoot, this show business. Yes, life is a crapshoot, but a dream is more of a crapshoot, Frank, because you risk everything for your dreams.

You feel like you can't miss, and maybe that's true, but one thing to know. Frank. Talent does not always rise to the top. It's like the world's best cannoli. Everybody wants a piece. And people in the business of entertainment are like medusas, Frank. What's a medusa? An animal, Frank. No, you can't beat it. It's mythical, Frank, like Godzilla, and it's got a million hands and it'll steal 'ya blind. And besides, you, you, you stupid you, I'm speaking metaphorically, as if to say, one cannot predict what life has in store because there are things in this world we can't control.

You see my point here, Frank, y'understand? 'Cause God forbid, I should discourage you. Yes? Good? All right? So, may we put this issue aside for the moment, Frank? Because I need to tell you something. What you do for the people in the neighborhood is very important, Frank. You bring sweetness into peoples' lives. I'm serious, Frank, a cannoli is a beautiful thing. And like a great aria, when it's finished, it can never be again. And yours, Frank, are the best. And for a man to be the best, that's something.

So live with that for now and who knows what the future may bring. All right? You-you-you monkey, you? And one more piece of advice. Don't live in the head, Frankie, live in the heart. So. Here's what I want you to do. I want you should walk down the stairs. Ya have a token? Get on the R train, uptown. Get off at Steinway. You know the stop? Good. Walk down the block. Get some flowers, keep walking. At the end of the block on the corner is a bakery. Frank's Bakery. Oh, you been there. Well, the girl behind the counter's named Marguerite? Recognize her? Good. Take her out somewhere nice, she's been neglected by her husband who thinks he's Frank Sinatra. She's looking very thin, lately, too, so get her a cannoli, fatten her up, okay?

Okay. So, we're finished here, Frank? With this issue? Yes? All right, you, you, you, leave me alone I've got work to do— but you know I'm here. Always, Frankie, when there's a problem I'm here. But regarding this issue, Frank, you know my feelings. So, get out of here, and don't forget: Life is full of wonderful things. Like cannoli! And Sinatra. And MARRIAGE, Frank. Your marriage. So go home to that lovely wife of yours, alright? She loves you. And I do, too. You do know that? KNOW that! All right?

Alright . . . Don't thank me, you had the answer before you walked in. So go, good-bye already. And bring me a cannoli next time, huh? And give Marguerite a big wet kiss from me, alright? What is it, Frank, spit it out. (*Pause.*) I love you, too, Frank. Frank? Get out your token, and GET OUT OF HERE you-you-you monkey, you!

Protection

JOHN WALCH

LANE sits on a stool with tweezers. He looks at a mini-reflection of himself in the band of his silver wedding ring. He brings tweezers to his left eyebrow and is about to pluck. Suddenly, he drops the tweezers, as if they had become a pair of hot tongs.

LANE: Pluck. Definition one: noun—courage, resolve, fortitude. (*He goes to pick up tweezers, but stops.*) As in: Lane hasn't the pluck to pick up a $9.99 pair of drugstore tweezers and pull out his mutant eyebrow.

It's not that I don't want to. I can't. Believe me, I wish I could. An eyebrow of this length is dangerous. It falls into my eye at inappropriate moments (in a meeting, in the line at the bank, while I'm driving) causing me to tear up . . . I find myself crying uncontrollably a lot lately. But, nevertheless, I can't participate in any more pain or loss, not even the loss of a single eyebrow. (*Shift.*)

Pluck. Definition two: verb—strum, pick, twang. As in: My wife plucked my curiosity when she went to a Russian peasant named Olga at twenty dollars a month to get her eyebrows shaped.

I'm not a controlling man, I'm not a suspicious husband. I don't go through the Visa bill with a highlighter marking questionable charges. BUT, I am an aware man, careful with money. I do glance at the credit card bills and when a name like "Hair Today Gone Tomorrow!" shows up, it's hard not to trip over a pun so low. And when it shows up not once, not twice, but month after month, well even a non-controlling and non-suspicious husband might ask his wife: "Hey, what's this place: Hair Today Gone Tomorrow! all about?"

And his wife responds: "Why is Greenland an island and Australia a continent?" Our code for evasion. Our inside joke for: "I don't know and/or please don't ask." But I press and that's when I find out about Olga.

My wife goes, went, to a Russian cosmetics specialist who would yank out her eyebrows. Mel knew we couldn't really afford another monthly expense, but she claimed: "The pain is exquisite, this woman's hands, Lane, they're strong peasant hands, and I know I can do it myself, but I feel nervous and weirdly self-conscious about shaping my own eyebrows. But when Olga does it, I feel totally at ease." I was astonished. We'd been married for four years and I never knew she did anything to her eyebrows—I thought they just came that way.

Pluck. Definition three: verb—pull out, yank. As in: To save twenty dollars a month I began to pluck my wife's eyebrows.

There's a lot to learn.

Bullet: Use good tweezers

Bullet: Pluck after a bath when the skin is warm

Bullet: Hold tweezers at 45-degree angle, pluck in the direction of the hair growth

Bullet: Follow the natural shape of the brow

Bullet: Apply tea bag to plucked area to reduce inflammation

Why Melanie allowed me to pluck her eyebrows is a question open to debate, how good I was at it is open to even further debate (although after she coached me, Mel swore I was better than Olga). What's not debatable is what it came to mean. The ritual.

Once a month, we'd turn off the ringers on all the phones and, while I was out renting a movie and picking up takeout, she'd bathe. Then, we'd settle for the night and she'd lift her eyes to me. They're big and green, peaceful islands floating in this sea of white.

Pluck. "Don't pull so hard. Firm, not hard." Pluck. "Careful not to take out too much, you'll leave me with a bald spot." Pluck. Pluck. Eyebrow after eyebrow after eyebrow. Half the time we wouldn't even watch the movie, we'd just talk. It didn't matter about what, because after looking into her eyes for an hour or two, studying the shape of her face, even the most lowbrow conversations became sacred. And sometimes we'd go to that place beyond words. Pluck. Pluck. Pluck. This is what I miss. (*Tears up slightly. He brushes it off and continues.*)

I'm sorry. I told you this mutant eyebrow falls in at bad times. But, I just can't. Oh, I hear what everybody says: "He should be over it by now." "It's been almost two years." But I'm not ready. It'll fall out on its own, when it's ready. Before that, before I'm ready, there's no reason to pluck it out.

Pluck. Definition four: verb—take away, forcibly remove. As in: My wife was plucked from this life too early.

It's raining on the highway. A car skids across the median and into our lane. I swerve. A semi from behind slams into the passenger door. An explosion of steel and steam. But I walk away. Open the door as if coming home from a normal work day. They say I was in shock, disoriented. I think they say this to make me feel better. They also say that there was probably nothing I could have done. Probably. I'm looking for Mel. Wandering all over the interstate shouting her name. It never once occurs to me: she's still in the car. Until . . . sirens, ambulances, fireman, a crowd of spectators. (*Picks up the tweezers.*)

A monstrous pair of tweezers appears on the scene. Men pry the car apart with these tweezers, these jaws of life. And I'm in their face, grabbing at their tweezers: "DON'T PULL SO HARD! GIVE IT TO ME! LET ME DO IT! I KNOW HOW TO DO THIS!" A paramedic yanks me away and sits me down. A gash in my head, blood all over my face, but I don't notice. The eyebrows, that's what they're for. To keep blood, sweat, rain from dripping in our eye. (*Sets tweezers down.*) For protection.

Wichita

HANK WILLENBRINK

A cheap hotel hallway. Marie, a woman Jackson has picked up at a bar, lies naked and crying. JACKSON enters the hall and speaks to her.

JACKSON: I wasn't tryin' to hurt . . . you ain't the only one. All right? You ain't the only one! I got 'em too—marks all over myself. That don't make it wrong—it's what happens when you love someone. Somethin's gotta hurt.

My dad taught me how to bait a hook—he took me out to the stock pond and pushed that worm down on the end . . . guts popped out all over the place. It hurt the worm . . . I wasn't tryin' to do that—(*She begins to cry.*)

No, don't start that cryin' again. No one's gonna hear ya; they're all asleep. The whole hotel. This is between us. No one believes you when you're naked. Don't—don't—don't fuck this up by wailin' all over the place.

It's yer eyebrows fault this started! Yeah, they stuck right outta the crowd, like little worms on a hook. Dad used to say you can always tell what kind of a girl she is by her eyebrows. How they curl up, does she take care of them? You do. I can tell. You take good care of yourself, why do you think I won't—

I'm sorry, all right. I touch rough, cause—you gotta let a woman know you love 'em. I wanna show you—come on . . . come on . . . we'll go back in the room. It'll be okay, I'll caress. I swear. You don't gotta get dressed—we'll take a shower. They got that smelly soap and we'll get wet. All over. Wet and— come here, I need to touch you. (*He reaches out. She backs away.*)

Don't start that! I'm trying to talk to you—fuck—I can't show you how I love you if'n I don't touch you. It's part of love. It's—Come here! Don't fuckin' run away from me again. Don't try it. I'll mark you more. You don't want that. Here! (*He grabs her.*) Yeah. Yeah. Don't fuck this up for me. Don't— I'm gonna get you underwater. Girls like it underwater. Everyone does, everything glistens, it's all shiny and rolly and pretty. Water does that to your body.

Daddy always liked it when I was in the shower—he said my body was pretty and shiny and he never touched rough there—he blamed it on the water. (*Beat.*) You're pretty, too. Just like I was.

Biographies

Paul Austin's (*Dreaming Angel*) professional life in the theatre spans forty years and includes acting and directing on and Off-Broadway, in regional theatres around the nation and acting for television and film. He has written plays, poetry, and essays for and about the theatre. His produced plays include *Artificial Light, Promises to Keep, Late Night Conspiracies, Quietus,* and *The Funny Men Are in Trouble.* His *Three Dream Plays* were recently published in *Newport Review 4X4.* He has recently finished a book about acting, *Spontaneous Behavior—The Art of Character Acting.* He is also the artistic director of the Image theatre and a member of Ensemble Studio Theatre. In addition to his professional career, Mr. Austin teaches acting and directing at Sarah Lawrence College.

Barton Bishop (*Competence*) is a Florida native whose plays include *The Amphibian Song, The Complex, For the Benefit of Mr. Bracket, God's Daughter, The Great Who Knows,* and *Plastic Castles.* He has also written several children's musicals for the New York Hall of Science. His work has been produced in Manhattan, Los Angeles, and Florida, where he has been the recipient of the Florida Playwright's Process award three times. He is currently a graduate student in the Department of Dramatic Writing at NYU's Tisch School of the Arts.

Errol Bray (*Monologue for a Rhino*) is an Australian playwright, director, and teacher who also works in and writes for youth theatre. His plays have been produced in all states in Australia and in Canada, the U.S., and Yugoslavia. Major plays—*The Choir* (on the theme of oppression through the symbol of the castration of choir boys) and *Nijinsky at Twilight* (a three-hander using dialogue, dance, and music to explore Nijinsky's madness)—have received acclaimed productions. His latest play, *Rhino* (two men trying to deal with masculinity issues), received development through Sydney's Mardi Gras Festival. He is the author of *Playbuilding* (published in the U.S. by Heinemann) about group devising of plays. He is Founding Patron of World Interplay—the international festival of young playwrights.

Mattias Brunn (*is this it?*) is an actor and playwright. He is the artistic director for the Atelier Theatre in Gothenburg, Sweden.

Aaron Cabell (*Whalespeak*) freelances as an actor and director. His most recent appearance as an actor was at the Clarence Brown Theatre in Knoxville, TN, as the magician, Alcandre, in Tony Kushner's adaptation of *The Illusion*. Other regional theatre appearances include Studio Arena Theatre, Pennsylvania Shakespeare Festival, North Carolina Shakespeare Festival, Virginia Stage Company, Vermont Stage Company, The Arden Theatre, and Philadelphia Festival Theatre for New Plays. Aaron has directed at the Virginia Stage Company (Pearl Cleage's *Blues for an Alabama Sky*); University of Tennessee, Knoxville (Gary Garrison's *The Big Fat Naked Truth*); Bloomsburg University (Imra Glodstein's *Oedipus Tyrannos*); and The University of Buffalo (*Twelfth Night* and Euripides' *Electra*). As a guest artist, Cabell has also directed, taught, and/or acted at Virginia Commonwealth University, University of Northern Iowa, Juniata College, and Studio Arena Theatre School.

Chong Tze Chien (*The Actor*) graduated from the Theatre Studies Programme of the National University of Singapore in 1999, after which he was appointed Associate Playwright of The Necessary Stage. He is currently the Company Playwright. He wrote the 1998 Singapore Dramatist Award Winning play, *PIE*, which was subsequently staged by TheatreWorks(S) Ltd in 1999. He also co-wrote *sex.violence .blood.gore* (with Alfian Sa'at) and *One Hundred Years in Waiting* (with Kuo Pao Kun and Haresh Sharma) for the 2001 Singapore Arts Festival. His other works include *Lift My Mind* for *Brainstorm (what's that in your head?)*, *Is This Our Stop?* for *M1 Youth Connection 2000,* and *Princess Diana is Dead* for *3Some* and *Spoilt* by The Necessary Stage. Tze Chien was the editor for *The Programme,* a quarterly free arts-zine published by the company. He participated in Interplay '99 in Australia, and represented Singapore for Playwright's Web 2000, a joint project between the Arts Centre in Calgary and The Necessary Stage, besides participating in other international playwriting exchanges. He also sits on the board of directors for The Finger Players Ltd, a local puppetry theatre company. His first collection of plays, *PIE to SPOILT,* was published by The Necessary Stage at the end of 2002.

Aaron Coates (*The Paper Bag*) is a playwright and an actor. His plays include *Pratfall, Modern Cowboys,* and *Good Old Days*. His most recent play, *The End of the Rope,* was short-listed for the 2002 Writers Guild of Alberta Award for Drama. As an actor, Coates has appeared in *Moliere, Good, Much Ado About Nothing, The Comedy of Errors,* and *Richard III*. In 2001, Coates traveled to Townsville, Australia, as a

Canadian delegate for World Interplay, the International Festival of Young Playwrights. Currently, he is an Apprentice Playwright at Alberta Theatre Projects. He lives in Calgary, Canada.

Dean Corrin (*Longing*) is a member of the Victory Gardens Playwrights Ensemble and chair of the Theatre Studies Department at The Theatre School, DePaul University. Four of his plays—*Battle of the Bands, Expectations, Butler County,* and *Gentrification*—have premiered at Victory Gardens. His plays have also been produced by the Tacoma Actors Guild, Addison Center Theatre (Texas), Stage #1 (Dallas), the Actors Theatre of St. Paul, Northlight Repertory, Missouri Repertory, New York StageWorks, and the Cape Cod Festival of New American Plays. His play, *Threadheads* (a musical for young audiences about Mother Jones and the child labor movement), was commissioned by DePaul University and premiered by Chicago Playworks. It was subsequently presented at the Bonderman National Youth Theatre Playwriting Symposium. Corrin served as literary manager for two seasons at the St. Nicholas Theatre Company. He lives in Chicago with his wife, Judy, and daughters, Julia and Ann. He is a member of the Dramatists Guild.

Dan Dietz (*a bone close to my brain*) is a playwright and actor living in Austin, Texas. His plays include *Dirigible, Blind Horses, Tilt Angel,* and *Temp Odyssey;* they have been seen in New York, Los Angeles, Seattle, Wilmington, Austin, and elsewhere. Awards and honors include a James A. Michener Playwriting Fellowship, three Austin Critics Table Awards for acting and playwriting, the Academy Theatre/Kennesaw State New Play Award, and a playwriting residency at the Millay Colony for the Arts. Dietz has been a featured writer in national workshops such as Hot House (Annex Theatre, Seattle), Play Labs (The Playwrights' Center, Minneapolis), and the New South for the New Century Festival (Horizon Theatre, Atlanta). He holds an MFA in Playwriting from the University of Texas at Austin.

Anton Dudley (*Jonathon and Stuart*) is a playwright, teacher, and director. His plays include *Slag Heap, The Lake's End, Soul Perversions, Spamlet, January 1, 2000,* and *Davy and Stu.* His works have been produced in New York, Massachusetts, Washington, DC, Los Angeles, and New Hampshire. Dudley is a recipient of the 2002 Manhattan Theatre Club Playwriting Fellowship and a 2001 Dramatists Guild Fellowship, as well as NYU's Goldberg Award and John Golden Prize in Playwriting. Dudley holds an MFA in Dramatic Writing from NYU and a BA in Drama from Vassar College. He is adjunct faculty in the Department of Dramatic Writing, Tisch School of the Arts, New York University; and in the Theatre Department at Adelphi University. Dudley is a member of the Dramatists Guild and is a Usual Suspect at New York Theatre Workshop. He also serves as literary manager for Cherry Red Productions in Washington, DC.

Chris Dunkley (*Darren*) is a Ph.D. student at the University of Exeter in England. *Mirita* won the 2001 PMA Writing Award and was produced at the Cherry Lane Theatre in New York and the Finborough Theatre in London. *The Devil's Pumpkins* won the 2002 International Student Playscript Competition. He is currently rewriting a trilogy of school plays about Kosovo.

Ben Ellis (*The Exhibit*) is an Australian playwright whose plays include *Post Felicity* (Currency Press) produced by Playbox Theatre Company, Melbourne, and *Outpatients,* which played in both Melbourne and Sydney. He has won several awards for new writing for the stage, including the national Patrick White Playwrights Award. A trio of (much longer) interrelated monologues set over a weekend, *Eclipses,* recently premiered in Melbourne. The Sydney Theatre Company has commissioned him to write a play, *These People,* investigating Australia's uniquely harsh treatment of asylum-seekers. He is a member of the Australian Writers Guild.

Jeffery Scott Elwell (*The Night We Met*) is a playwright, artistic director, and educator. His published plays include *The Art of Dating, Evening Education, Dead Fish, Stepping Out, Escape from Bondage, Being Frank, An Ordinary Morning,* and *Violent Images.* His works have been produced throughout the United States as well as in Australia, Canada, and Sweden. He is the recipient of a Mississippi Arts Commission Playwriting Fellowship, a Tennessee Williams Scholarship, a Nebraska Arts Commission Fellowship for Playwriting, and an NEH Summer Seminar Fellowship. He has received $229,000 in grants and fellowships during his career. Elwell holds a Ph.D. from Southern Illinois University at Carbondale. He is professor and chair in the Department of Theatre Arts at the University of Nebraska. Elwell is a member of the Dramatists Guild.

Nate Eppler (*How to Quit Properly*) is a playwright and actor currently living in Nashville and Memphis. His first play, *Vote Jesus,* premiered Off-Off-Off (etc.) Broadway at the Acting Studio in New York. His play *Keeping Up with the Joneses* was the runner-up for the 2002 Kennedy Center American College Theatre Festival New Play Award. Eppler is a founding member of the Breezeway Theatre Company and a proud member of the amazing Giggle Jones sketch comedy troupe.

Robert Ford (*She's Material*) writes, directs, and teaches in Fayetteville, Arkansas, where he is an artist-in-residence at the Walton Arts Center/Nadine Baum Studios. Among other distinctions, his first play, *Tierra del Fuego,* won the Stanley Drama Award and an alternate slot in the Chesterfield Film Company Competition. His play *The Fall of the House* (formerly, *Final Poe*) was selected for the Harvest Festival of New American Plays at the State Theater in Austin and was a finalist in the Morton R. Sarett National Playwriting Competition. A one-act, *Manhattan Transaction,* was among those chosen Best of Fest by the producers of Frontera Fest in Austin, and it appears in *Poems & Plays.* Ford's fiction has been published in *American Short Fiction* and his first novel, *The Student Conductor,* is forthcoming from Penguin Putnam. He holds an MFA in Playwriting and Screenwriting from the Michener Center for Writers, University of Texas at Austin, and an MFA in Acting from Rutgers.

David Frank (*Prenatal Paralysis*) is the author of five plays, three of which have been produced in New York City: *Address Unknown, In the Company of Strangers, Stolen Moments, Bury Me at Sea,* and *The Sheriff.* His first feature-length screenplay, *59th Street Bridge,* is currently in development. Frank's film roles include Baxter in Nevil Dwek's recently completed *Undermind,* Robert in Benno Schoeberth's *Shelter,* Todd Komarnicki's upcoming *Achilles Heart* with Paul Rudd, *A Perfect Murder* with Michael Douglas, Matt Mahurin's *Mugshot,* and the Bronx reggae western *Comeback.* He co-produced and acted in Chris Robertson's short film, *A Change of Climate,* starring Victor Argo, which was selected for the Independent Feature Film Market in New York, as well as the Montclair Film Festival, the Nashville Film Festival, and the Exground Film Festival in Wiesbaden, Germany. Frank was a founding member of both The Art and Work Ensemble Theatre, where he acted, directed, artistic directed, wrote, and taught. He is now, as playwright and actor, a member of Circle Rep's offshoot company, Circle East. His numerous theatre acting credits include the New York premiere of John Lahr's *The Manchurian Candidate;* Jason Katim's *The Man Who Couldn't Dance;* and the AWE's productions of *120 Seconds, Romeo and Juliet,* and *Present Laughter.*

Jason T. Garrett (*Lunch*) holds an MFA in Dramatic Writing from New York University's Tisch School of the Arts, an MA in Drama from The Catholic University of America, and a BA in English and Theatre from the University of Tennessee at Knoxville. Jason has had readings or productions of his plays at Expanded Arts (NYC), Soho Rep (NYC), the Schaeberle Studio (NYC), Tisch School of the Arts (NYC), Source Theatre (DC), the National Theatre (DC), Hartke Theatre (DC), the American College Theatre Festival (Most Promising Playwright, 1996), Clarence Brown Theatre Lab (TN), Oak Ridge Playhouse (TN), Louisiana Tech University, and the University of Tennessee.

Gary Garrison (*Take a Load Off*) is the artistic director, producer, and a member of the full-time faculty in the Department of Dramatic Writing Program at NYU's Tisch School of the Arts. He has produced the last fifteen Festivals of New Works for NYU, working with hundreds of playwrights, directors, and actors. Garrison's plays include *Padding the Wagon, Rug Store Cowboy, Cherry Reds, Gawk, Oh Messiah Me, We Make a Wall, The Big Fat Naked Truth, Scream with Laughter, Smoothness with Cool, Empty Rooms, Does Anybody Want a Miss Cow Bayou?* and *When a Diva Dreams*. His work has been featured at Primary Stages, The Directors Company, Manhattan Theatre Source, StageWorks, Fourth Unity, Open Door Theatre, African Globe Theatre Company, Pulse Ensemble Theatre, Expanded Arts, and New York Rep. He is the author of the critically acclaimed *The Playwright's Survival Guide: Keeping the Drama in Your Work and Out of Your Life* (Heinemann), *Perfect Ten: Writing and Producing the Ten-Minute Play* (Heinemann) and co-editor of the first volume of *Monologues for Men by Men* (Heinemann) with Michael Wright. He is a member of the Dramatists Guild.

Graham Gordy (*Barry, the Human Sponge*) recently completed his MFA in Dramatic Writing from NYU's Tisch School of the Arts. He is a member of the Royal Court Theatre's Young Writer's Programme and took part in the World Interplay International Festival of Young Playwrights. Gordy was published in the last *Monologues for Men by Men* and is proud to be part of this one. He hails from Toadsuck, Arkansas, and is a member of the Dramatists Guild.

Jon Haller (*In the Arboretum*) is a twenty-two-year-old writer from Carbondale, Illinois. In the past two years, his plays *Lusona* and *Duel* were workshopped and read at the John F. Kennedy Center in

Washington, DC. *Lusona* received its premiere in June 2002 at the Bailiwick Theater in Chicago under the direction of Alexis Williams. He has received two fellowships from the Kennedy Center and is currently seeking an MFA from York University in Toronto. He is a member of the Dramatists Guild.

Mats Hellerstedt-Thorin (*The Pain of Passion*) was born in 1958, and started acting professionally in 1979. Trained as an actor in London, he lives and works with the theatre as an actor, director, writer, improvisation teacher and fight director in Sweden. Improvisation is at the heart of his work and also his life. Since 1990 he has been a permanent member of Atelierteatern, the oldest small group theatre in Europe. Before that Mats worked at Wasa Theatre in Finland and all over Sweden as a freelance professional.

Robert Henry (*Drinking with Dad*) is a writer living in Los Angeles. His work can currently be seen in *American Profile* magazine and heard on the syndicated radio show *Little Known Facts* (and seen in that show's accompanying book). In the past he's written everything from street theater for what is now *Dollywood* to personalized psychic predictions.

Vishakan Jeyakumar (*'Lac*) was born in Sri Lanka and raised in New Zealand. He is a graduate student at the Department of Dramatic Writing at NYU's Tisch School of the Arts. His one-act play *Arranged Marriage* was performed in the department's theatre as part of the Festival of New Works 2002. His full-length play *Amritsar* was co-winner of the Goldberg Prize for Playwriting (2002). Jeyakumar would like to thank his parents and brother for their continued support, and Gary Garrison for being an inspirational teacher and for giving him this opportunity.

Moshe Kasher (*Look Before You Leap*) was born in 1979 in New York and was raised in Oakland, California. He is currently a student at the University of California at Santa Barbara, where his work has been produced and performed by the BFA Theatre Program's Annual Monologue Festival. His work tends to address the theme of identity: religious, sexual, personal, or otherwise. His latest work focuses on the issues of Jewish intermarriage.

Kipp Koenig (*Down for the Count*) is a screenwriter and librettist currently living in New York City with his wife and daughter. He has written numerous screenplays and musical librettos and received a BFA in Musical Theatre Performance from The University of Michigan. He is a member of the Dramatists Guild.

Paul Lambrakis (*Family Man*) received his MFA in 1998 from the Department of Dramatic Writing at New York University's Tisch School of the Arts. Since then, he has written for several television productions, including PAX TV's *Destination Stardom* and Telemundo's *Sueños de Fama*. In addition to developing his own screenplays, he currently freelances as a writer/producer for the *Discover America* travel series, which airs on The Travel Channel. The travelogues feature small towns across America and in the Caribbean as vacation destinations. He has also written several segments for a new PBS series entitled *Voices of Vision*. These highlight different nonprofit organizations and the work they perform.

Ken Ludwig (*Shakespeare in Hollywood*) is the author of several Broadway, Off-Broadway, and West End plays and musicals. *Lend Me a Tenor* was produced in London by Andrew Lloyd Webber and nominated for the Olivier Award as Comedy of the Year. On Broadway, it was directed by Jerry Zaks and nominated for the Tony Award for Best Play. *Crazy for You* ran for years in London and New York, won the Olivier and Tony Awards for Best Musical, and was broadcast nationwide on PBS Television's "Great Performances." *Moon Over Buffalo* marked Carol Burnett's triumphant return to Broadway after thirty years; she was followed in the role by Lynn Redgrave. In London, it played at the Old Vic and starred Joan Collins and Frank Langella. Ludwig's latest plays are *Leading Ladies,* a comedy in the tradition of *Some Like It Hot; Twentieth Century,* a new adaptation of the Hecht-MacArthur classic; and *Shakespeare in Hollywood,* commissioned by The Royal Shakespeare Company and recently presented at the Kennedy Center in Washington. Other works include *Sullivan & Gilbert* (Kennedy Center), *The Adventures of Tom Sawyer* (Broadway musical), *Postmortem* (Off-Broadway play), and *All Shook Up* (a screenplay for producer-director Frank Oz). He is a founding member of the Shakespeare Theatre of Washington, DC, and has served on the New Play Committees of the National Endowment for the Arts and the American College Theater Festival.

Todd McCullough (*Male Pattern*) is a playwright and screenwriting student at UCLA. His plays include *Local Celebrities, Forever Blue,* and *Rainy Day People*. He has won several awards, including the Kennedy Center's Mark Twain Comedy Playwriting Award (for *Rainy Day*

People). *Local Celebrities* is being published by Dramatic Publishing Co. in an anthology of student-written plays. McCullough currently lives in Los Angeles.

Carlos Murillo's (*The Crafty Baboon*) plays include *Mimesophobia* (or *Before and After*), *A Human Interest Story* (or *The Gory Details and All*), *Offspring of the Cold War, Patron Saint of the Nameless Dead, Schadenfreude, Near Death Experiences with Leni Riefenstahl, Never Whistle While You're Pissing,* and *Subterraneans.* They have been produced at Walkabout Theatre in Chicago; Circle X in Los Angeles; En Garde Arts, Soho Rep, and Nada, Inc. in New York City; The Group Theatre in Seattle; and Red Eye Collaboration in Minneapolis. His plays have been developed at A.S.K. Theatre Projects, the New York Shakespeare Festival New Work Now! Festival, Sundance, the Bay Area Playwrights Festival, PlayLabs at the Playwrights Center in Minneaopolis, Annex Theatre in Seattle, Lincoln Center, New York Theatre Workshop, and South Coast Repertory Company. Murillo is the recipient of a 1996 Minnesota State Arts Board Cultural Collaborations Grant; the 1996 National Latino Playwriting Award; a 1995–1996 Jerome Fellowship at the Playwrights' Center; and commissions from the Public, South Coast Rep, and En Garde Arts. *Schadenfreude* was recently published in the Winter/Spring 2002 issue of TheatreForum's *International Theatre Journal.* He has taught at the Theatre School of DePaul University and Barat College in Lake Forest, Illinois.

Joel Murray (*Gone*) has written, directed, and acted in approximately 150 stage, film, prime time, and daytime television productions including national commercials. He has been a member of numerous theatre groups, such as the MET Theatre with actors and Oscar winners Ed Harris and Holly Hunter and Tony winner James Gammon. He has won numerous best actor and director awards, including a student Emmy for a project he co-wrote, and received numerous grants and fellowships for directing and playwriting. Murray has also presented numerous papers on acting, directing, playwriting, and theory and criticism at national and regional conferences and published papers in national, regional, and international journals. Further, he has sold and optioned screenplays. In addition to teaching at various universities such as California State University and Purdue University at Fort Wayne, Joel taught acting in Los Angeles with well-known professionals including Alan Vint and Tom Bower.

Matthew Nader (*Drug Rep*) has been called "America's Best New Writer" by his mother. He is currently finishing a film degree at the University of Tulsa. This monologue is excerpted from a screenplay entitled *Tulsa.*

Brian Nelson (*Double*) is a playwright, television writer, director, and dramaturg. His plays include *Overlooked, Radiant, Secret Ballot, Consolation,* and *Marilyn in Repertory.* His television credits include *JAG, Lois and Clark, Earth: Final Conflict, So Weird, In a Heartbeat, Vanishing Son,* the German television series *Wolffs Revier,* and the ABC miniseries adaptation of *20,000 Leagues Under the Sea* starring Michael Caine. His directing credits include the Kennedy Center, the Mark Taper Forum Literary Cabaret, Woolly Mammoth Theatre Company, Round House Theatre, and the Texas Shakespeare Festival. During his tenure as literary manager for East West Players, he inaugurated the David Henry Hwang Writers Institute, and subsequently edited *Asian American Drama: Nine Plays from the Multiethnic Landscape* (Applause Books). His honors and awards include an Alfred P. Sloan/Ensemble Studio Theatre Fellowship, a Prism Award, an Ovation Award nomination for outstanding direction, and two Los Angeles Drama–Logue Awards. He holds degrees from Yale University and the University of California, Los Angeles, and currently teaches in the School of Theatre at the University of Southern California. He is a member of the Freedom to Write Committee of PEN Center USA West and of the Writers Guild of America.

Dan Nielsen (*A Joke on the New Guy*) is a poet and playwright. His poems have appeared in several major anthologies including *Stand Up Poetry* (University of Iowa Press), *The Random House Treasury of Light Verse,* and *Created Writing: Poetry from New Angles* (Prentice Hall). His plays include *Waiting for the Weinermobile, Andor & Nantzi,* and *A Myoclonic Jerk.* He also works in radio as a scriptwriter for WPR's *Hotel Milwaukee.*

Adrian Page (*Just Do It*) is twenty-nine years old and lives in East London, where he was born. He studied theatre at Goldsmiths College and spent three years with the Royal Court Young Writer's Programme, where he was selected to represent the UK at Interplay Australia. In 1998, Adrian established Pear Shaped Productions, a company dedicated to producing new writing in London and beyond. The company was selected for the National Student Drama Festival 2000, and also traveled to Slovakia to perform at the Istrapolitana Festival. Since 2000, he has been Writer in Residence at the Half Moon Young

People's Theatre, which has commissioned him for a new play that toured in Autumn 2002. He is also a freelance director and teaches drama at the CityLit adult college in central London, and Greenwich Arts. He strives to challenge form in order to create imaginative and poetic theatre, inspired by the mediocrity of urban living, the meretriciousness of consumerist culture, and the mendacity of modern government. Plays include: *Between the Fourth and the Fifth* (White Bear, London; Istropolitana, Slovakia), *Armchair UK* (White Bear, Riverside Studios), *Who Wants to be the Disco King?* (Goldsmiths Studio, Stephen Joseph Theatre), *Subterfuge, Schtum* (LOST Theatre), and *Couch Potatoes* (Goldsmiths Studio, Dunedin Festival New Zealand).

Malcolm Pelles (*Panthers, Police, and Baby Mamas*) was born in North Carolina and raised in Silver Spring, Maryland. In 1999, he was a finalist in Young Playwrights Inc.'s National Playwriting Competition. He also wrote and directed *Representative Earl Harris,* a short film currently making its way around the national film festival circuit.

Arzhang Pezhman (*Scrap*) is a young playwright from England whose first play, *Local* (published by Aurora Metro), was produced and staged by the Royal Court Theatre in London. He has also worked as a freelance writer's tutor for the Royal Court on several occasions. He is currently working on a piece for the Birmingham REP Theatre, as well as developing a feature-length screenplay. Arzhang has an MA in Playwriting Skills from Birmingham University and lectures in script writing at Wolverhampton University in his hometown.

Richard Stockton Rand (*Vinnie G*) has acted on and Off-Broadway; in regional theatres in the United States, Europe, and Canada; and in films for public television. He has written and performed twelve one-person shows at sixty universities, theatres, and festivals and is the recipient of an Indiana Arts Commission–National Endowment for the Arts Artist Fellowship for solo performance. Recently published monologues include *I Dreamed I Was a Baseball Card* and *The Leap* in Heinemann's *Baseball Monologues.* He has also published dramatic work in *Sycamore Review, Hopewell Review: New Work by Indiana's Best Writers, Indiana Theatre Journal, Hyphen, Mobius,* and *Slipstream.* He is the current head of Undergraduate Theatre at Purdue University and president of the Association of Theatre Movement Educators.

Greg Romero (*The Eulogy*) is originally from Louisiana and is a cofounder and dramaturg for rm 120 theatre in Austin, Texas. Also an associate member of Literary Managers and Dramaturgs of the Americas, as well as Austin ScriptWorks, Romero has produced, directed, and/or dramaturged more than a dozen productions of new plays for rm 120 theatre. His own plays have been produced in Austin, Dallas, Fort Worth, and Natchitoches, Louisiana. Romero holds a B.A. in Liberal Arts from the Louisiana Scholars College.

Ari Roth (*Interview with a Pharmacist*) is artistic director of Theater J in Washington, DC, and author of *Born Guilty*, which is based on the book by Peter Sichrovsky; it was originally commissioned and produced by Arena Stage, directed by Zelda Fichandler, and presented Off-Broadway at the American Jewish Theater and in dozens of other productions across the country. Most recently he produced *Born Guilty* at Theater J in repertory with its sequel, *Peter and the Wolf*, commissioned by the National Foundation for Jewish Culture. *Goodnight Irene* was commissioned by Manhattan Theatre Club and has been produced at Performance Network in Michigan and Hypothetical Theatre Company in New York. Comedies include *Love & Yearning in the Not for Profits and Other Marital Distractions* and *Oh, The Innocents,* which have been produced at Theater J, Ensemble Studio Theater, and HB Playwrights Foundation. He was nominated for a Helen Hayes Award for *Life in Refusal*. He is a graduate of The University of Michigan, where he won two Hopwood Awards for playwriting, and has taught at The University of Michigan, Brandeis and New York University.

Brad Rothbart (*Rashid's Rant*) is a freelance actor, director, and dramaturg. Currently devoting his energies to New Play Development, he is dedicated to working with contemporary American playwrights who aim to stretch the boundaries of theatre through the use of experimental form and/or radical content. Previous theatrical ventures include five years creating and performing original works with The Living Theatre, as well as directing *We Who Have Read The Girl Detective* by V.F. Zialcita (loosely based on a story by Kelly Link) for the 2001 Philadelphia Fringe Festival. Rothbart's article, "*Ahistoricity,* Multiplicity and Velocity: Radical Discontinuity and its Effects on the Dramaturgical Process," was published by *TheatreForum* in its Summer/Fall 2002 issue. He recently dramaturged *The Shape Shifter* by R.L. Nesvet for the PlayWorks Program at the 2002 Association for Theatre in Higher Education (ATHE) Conference. Rothbart is a proud member of both LMDA (The Literary Managers and Dramaturgs of the Americas) and the RAT Conference.

Haresh Sharma (*sweet dream*) has been the resident playwright of The Necessary Stage since 1990. In 1994, he won a Shell/National Arts Council Scholarship to pursue an MA in Playwriting at the University of Birmingham, UK. To date, he has more than 40 full-length and short plays produced. His collaboration with The Necessary Stage's artistic director Alvin Tan has resulted in many acclaimed productions including *Lanterns Never Go Out; Those Who Can't, Teach; Pillars; Completely With/Out Character; Rosnah; ABUSE SUXXX!!!* and *godeatgod*. His play *Still Building* was performed in Cairo in 1992 for the Cairo Experimental Theatre Festival, in Glasgow for Mayfest 1994 and in London. In 1995, *There is No New Thing Under the Sun* was staged for Mayfest, by the Strathclyde Arts Centre. The Necessary Stage presented *Rosnah* in Melbourne in 1997, and *untitled women talk* was staged for the Macau Fringe Festival in 2000. In 1993, he was awarded the Singapore Literature Prize (Merit) for a collection of his plays, *Still Building*, which was also awarded the Singapore Book Prize (Merit) in 1996. Another collection, *This Chord and Others,* was published by Minerva Press in 1999. Ethos Books published his critically acclaimed *Off Centre*. He was the National Arts Council's Young Artist Award Winner for Drama in 1997.

Eugene Stickland (*Men of His Generation*) lives in Calgary, Canada, and is Alberta Theatre Projects' playwright in residence. Plays produced at ATP and elsewhere include *Some Assembly Required* (1994), *Sitting on Paradise* (1996), *A Guide to Mourning* (1998) and *Midlife* (2002). His work is produced frequently in theatres throughout Canada and occasionally in the U.S. Eugene devotes a lot of time and energy teaching and mentoring young playwrights in Calgary and as far away as Australia. He is currently working on a new play, *A Study in Concrete*.

Dan Stroeh (*Booker-T Is Back in Town*) is a graduate of Wittenberg University in Springfield, Ohio. Stroeh is a New York-based playwright whose plays include *The Second Advent, The Artist's Way, Law-V-Bowem,* and *Her*. Stroeh received the 2001 National Student Playwriting Award for his autobiographical one-man play, *it is no desert,* as part of the Kennedy Center/American College Theatre Festival's Michael Kanin Playwriting Awards Program. The Cincinnati Arts Association named him the Emerging Artist of the 2000–2001 season, and *it is no desert* also received third place recognition for the David Mark Cohen National Playwriting Award presented by The Association for Theatre in Higher Education. Stroeh has been a visiting artist at the Sundance Theatre Lab and the Mark Taper Forum's Other Voices Chautauqua 2001. He is the playwright-in-residence for the Alarm Clock Theatre Company of Boston and is a member of the Dramatists Guild.

Gary Sunshine's (*1 BR, Walk-In Kitchen*) play *Mercury* was produced by HERE Arts Center in association with Eve Ensler. His work has been seen and developed at MCC Theater, New York Theatre Workshop's Just Add Water Festival, the Underwood Theater, the New Group, The Flea, the Directors Company, the Cherry Lane Alternative, and Rising Phoenix Rep. His play *Al Takes a Bride* will be published in *The Best Short Plays of 2001* (Applause) and his play *The Leaks They Left* is a finalist for the 2002 Heideman Award. He is currently working as the writer of a documentary about a writing group at a women's maximum security prison. He is a member of the Dramatists Guild.

John Walch (*Protection*) is current artistic director of Austin Script Works and teaches playwriting at the University of Texas at Austin. His play *The Dinosaur Within* was awarded a grant from the Kennedy Center Fund for New American Plays and premiered at Austin's State Theater, where it was awarded the 2002 Austin Critic's Table Award for Outstanding Original Script. His solo piece, *Circumference of a Squirrel,* premiered at Austin's Zachary Scott Theater Center and was awarded the 2001 Austin Critic's Table Award for Outstanding Original Script. The play was subsequently produced by the Mark Taper Forum in Los Angeles and opened Off-Broadway at Urban Stages. Walch's plays have been developed through the Public Theater New Works Now Festival, A.S.K. Theatre Projects, Shenandoah International Playwright's Retreat, Playwright's Center of Minneapolis, the State Theater's Harvest Festival of New American Plays, WordBRIDGE Playwright's Lab, Play Works, and the New Work Festival at the Mark Taper Forum. Walch received the Marc Klein Playwriting Award for *Jesting with Edged Tools,* the 1997 Austin Critic's Table Award for *Craving Gravy,* and the 2000 Charlotte Woolard Award from the Kennedy Center recognizing a promising new voice in the American theater. Walch is the current Alfred P. Sloan playwriting fellow at Manhattan Theatre Club, where he is at work on a new play. He is a member of the Dramatists Guild.

Michel Wallerstein (*Last Farewell*) was born and raised in Lausanne, Switzerland, and came to New York in 1981; there he studied film at NYU and fell in love with the city. Plays include *Lap Dance* (Pulse Ensemble Theatre, Expanded Arts, Turnip Festival*), Five Women*

Waiting (Manhattan Theatre Source), *Boomerang* (Expanded Arts), *Off Hand* (Manhattan Theatre Source, Stage Works). *Off Hand* was also published in Gary Garrison's book, *Perfect Ten: Writing and Producing the Ten-Minute Play*. He writes television scripts, often with partner Linda Wendell, primarily for the European market. He is thrilled to be part of *Monologues for Men by Men, Volume Two,* having been published in the first volume.

Hank Willenbrink (*Wichita*) is currently studying theatre. His plays have been produced at the Kennedy Center/American College Theatre Festival and, most recently, World Interplay International Festival of Young Playwrights in Australia. One of his monologues is featured in *Monologues for Men by Men* (Heinemann). Willenbrink is from Toadsuck, Arkansas.

Michael Wright (*Sleeping, Son*) is an author and educator with extensive professional credits in writing for performance, as well as more than twenty years' teaching experience in undergraduate and graduate theatre. He is the Director of the Interdisciplinary Program in Creative Writing at The University of Tulsa. Wright is a national advisor to Austin Script Works Theatre; director/dramaturg for the WordBRIDGE Playwrights Laboratory; the U.S. representative to World Interplay Festival of Young Playwrights in Townsville, Australia; and an advisor to the Playwrights Cove of the Necessary Stage theatre in Singapore. His books include: *The Student's Guide to Playwriting Opportunities* (Theatre Directories, Inc.) and *Playwriting in Process* and *Playwriting Master Class* (Heinemann). He has co-edited the *Monologues for Men by Men* series for Heinemann with Gary Garrison of New York University. His plays, poems, fiction, and photography have appeared in *The Elvis Monologues, Scenes and Monologues for Mature Actors, Monologues from the Road, Rio Grande Review,* and *Voces Fronterizas,* among others. A former National Endowment for the Arts Playwriting Fellowship recipient, he is a member-at-large of the Governing Council for ATHE and a member of the Dramatists Guild.

Michael Yergin (*Grand People*) is a student in the NYU Tisch Department of Dramatic Writing at which his short play, *Death of a Salesman,* was recently produced in the Undergraduate Ten-Minute Play Festival. Hailing from Chicago, he studied at The Chicago Academy for the Arts and presented readings of his work at The Chicago Cultural Center; he also studied at Simon's Rock of Bard College, at which his play *The Mahogany Staircase* was produced.

Performance Rights

For Paul Austin, contact the author at *paustin@bestweb.net* or P.O. Box 324 Kauneonga Lake, NY 12749.

For Barton Bishop, contact the author at *bartonbishop@hotmail.com*.

For Errol Bray, contact the author at *errolbray@hotmail.com*.

For Mattias Brunn, contact the author at *mattias.brunn@telia.com*.

For Aaron Cabell, contact the author at *PlanckLength@aol.com*.

For Chong Tze Chien, contact the author at *tzechien@necessary.org*.

For Aaron Coates, contact the author at *aaronbcoates@hotmail.com*.

For Dean Corrin, contact the author at The Theatre School, DePaul University, 2135 N. Kenmore, Chicago, IL 60614-4111, or through his email at *dcorrin@depaul.edu*.

For Dan Dietz, contact the author at *dandietz@earthlink.net*.

For Anton Dudley, contact the author through Joan Scott, President, Joan Scott Management LLC, 12 West 72nd Street, #10D, New York, NY 10023; 212-362-0421; *jscott@joanscottllc.com*.

For Chris Dunkley, contact the author through Rose Cobbe, c/o Peters Fraser & Dunlop, Drury House, 34-43 Russell Street, London WC2B 5HA, U.K., *postmaster@pfd.co.uk*.

For Ben Ellis, contact the author through The Cameron Creswell Agency, Suite 5, 2 New McLean St., Edgecliff New South Wales, 2027, Australia.

For Jeffery Elwell, contact the author through Ann Farber, Farber Literary Agency, 14 East 75th Street, New York, NY 10021; 212-861-7075.

For Nate Eppler, contact the author at *raysmart@hotmail.com*.

For Bob Ford, contact the author at *bobaford@hotmail.com*.

For David Frank, contact the author through Maddie Perrone of Literary Artists Representatives, 575 West End Ave., #GRC, New York, NY 10024; 212-787-3808.

For Jason T. Garrett, contact the author at *www.JasonTGarrett.com*.

For Gary Garrison, contact the author through Fifi Oscard, Fifi Oscard Talent and Literary Agency, 100 W. 40th Street, New York, NY 10018; 212-784-1100; or the author's website at *www.garygarrison.com*.

For Graham Gordy, contact Howard Rosenstone, Rosenstone/Wender, 38 East 29th Street, 10th Floor, New York, NY 10016; 212-725-9445.

For Jon Haller, contact the author at *jonhaller@hotmail.com.*

For Mats Hellerstedt-Thorin, contact the author at *matsthorin@hotmail.com.*

For Robert Henry, contact the author at *3b@compuserve.com.*

For Vishakan Jeyakumar, contact the author at *VISHAKAN7@hotmail.com.*

For Moshe Kasher, contact the author at *moshekasher@hotmail.com.*

For Kipp Koenig, contact the author at *Kipp.Koenig@gs.com.*

For Paul Lambrakis, contact the author at *pwlambson@aol.com.*

For Ken Ludwig, contact the author through Peter Franklin at The Gersh Agency, 212-634-8124.

For Todd McCullough, contact the author at *wywrite@yahoo.com.*

For Carlos Murillo, contact the author through Morgan Jeness, c/o Helen Merrill, Ltd., 295 Lafayette St., New York, NY 10012.

For Joel Murray, contact the author at *jmurray@utep.edu.*

For Matthew Nader, contact the author at *matthew-nader@utulsa.edu.*

For Dan Nielsen, contact the author at *Ventorpent@prodigy.net.*

For Brian Nelson, contact the author through Jonathan Westover, The Gage Group,14724 Ventura Blvd., Suite 505, Sherman Oaks, CA 91403; 818-905-3800.

For Adrian Page, contact the author at *pearshapedprod@hotmail.com.*

For Malcolm Pelles, contact the author at *mjpelles@hotmail.com.*

For Arzhang Pezhman, contact the author through Nick Marston, Curtis Brown Agency, Haymarket House, 4th floor, 28/29 Haymarket, London SW1Y 4SP; phone 020 7360 7389.

For Richard Stockton Rand, contact the author at *richrand@purdue.edu.*

For Greg Romero, contact the author at *gregoryromero@yahoo.com.*

For Ari Roth, contact the author through Susan Schulman, Susan Schulman Agency, 454 W. 44th Street, New York, NY 10036; 212-713-1633; *Schulman@aol.com.*

For Brad Rothbart, contact the author at *scrdchao@comcast.net.*

For Haresh Sharma, contact the author at *haresh@necessary.org.*

For Eugene Stickland, contact the author at *eugenius@telusplanet.net.*

For Dan Stroeh, contact the author at *DanStroeh@aol.com.*

For Gary Sunshine, contact the author through John B. Santoianni, 275 Seventh Avenue, 26th Floor, New York, NY 10001; 646-486-4600.

For John Walch, contact the author through John Buzzetti, The Gersh Agency, 130 W. 42nd Street, Suite 2300, New York, NY 10036.

For Michel Wallerstein, contact the author at *MICHELWALLERSTEIN@yahoo.com.*

For Hank Willenbrink, contact the author at *hankwillenbrink @yahoo.com.*

For Michael Wright, contact the author at *myquagga@yahoo.com.*

For Michael Yergin, contact the author at *my301@nyu.edu.*